PROGrAMME

Introduction 1

ACT I: BELL PEPPER: SOCIAL SITUATIONS 13

Fleurtation 15
Antisocializing 23
Unrequitia 33
Homo Swipian 43
Senescention 51
Pinnaclascention 61
Binocusaurus 75

ACT II: JALAPEÑO: DIVERSE RANTS 85

Nomenclusion 87
Mellifluey 99
Misogynicely 111
Maladvice 121
Econominus 129
Addictapologist 141
Quantititty 155

ANTIPROGENITICS 169

INTERMISSIONARY 179

ACT III: HABANERO: CONCEPTION OF REALITY 185

HYPOTHESCIENT 187
SOMNETICS 199
METAMETACOGNITION 211
EXISTENTIA 225
TEMPORALUMINESCENCE 237
RELIGIOPHOBIA 249

ACT IV: BHUT JOLOKIA: PERMISSION OF DEATH ... 257

VEGANISMISMS 259
MEDIAREALISM 269
NOTRACISTBUT 277
ENVIRONMISANTHROPY 289
POLITICUE 297
UTILITARIOFASCISM 313

EPILOGIC 327

words that set the tone

INTRODICTION

Coffee Shop

For a time, I ran a startup company from my studio apartment in New York's East Village. My daily routine was to wake up naturally, spend an hour in bed checking email, choose a pair of pants off the floor, and ideally be out the door by noon on my way to one of my neighborhood coffee shops in the hopes of getting in a few hours of focused work instead of wasting time writing.

One day, for the mere sake of change, I decided to walk to a more *distant* coffee shop. It was the middle of winter and was snowing, but I made the trek.

I arrived at the café, the Blue Bottle on Clinton St., and ordered an espresso over ice, my go-to coffee shop order. I found an open table, took my seat, began mentally preparing for a day of productivity, and on the table, I saw two fruit flies...

Fucking.

That startled me. Have you ever walked in on people having sex? It was a miniature version of that feeling. Like, *Whoa, sorry! I thought this door was the bathroom. But lock the door next time, would ya?!*

To be honest, it hadn't occurred to me that fruit flies fuck. Of course, they must. They multiply like, well, fruit flies. But what really got me thinking was the position they had been employing.

Doggy style.

INTRODUCTION

I'm not sure what else I expected. Had I walked in on them performing reverse cowgirl or advanced Kamasutra, I surely would have called the Entomological Society to take them in for observation. Because, now that I thought about it, it seemed to me that *all animals do it doggy style*. Water buffalos, emus, spotted leopards, bats; they're all hittin' it from the back!

How fascinating, I thought. I had another sip of my frigid espresso.

Why, then, *did* doggy style get named such? Doggies don't have a monopoly on the position—not by a long shot! Canines, I theorized, just happen to be the species *we* most often walk in on having sex. So, we carelessly named the position after our best friend.

Humans do it *doggy* too, of course. However, I would have to call it a bit of a novelty for us. It's not our go-to, not our default in the way it is for every other species. If anything, we're the Darwinian freaks in the sack with our signature style, our prolific practice of *the missionary position*.

So, given doggy style's near-ubiquity among terrestrial beings, I say we rename the position something *neutral*, something *standard*, something *boring* to reflect just how commonplace it is across the animal kingdom. Something like... *per usual*.

Turn over, baby, let's do it per usual.

And let's give *missionary* the new name it deserves: *human style*.

INTRODUCTION

Preempting Criticism

At the time of this writing, my claim to fame is null. I'm exactly nobody. My area of expertise is a similarly empty set. I'm not an expert in anything. Nor am I the kind of person whose story you'd love to know.

This book has no central point, no main take-away, no unifying message. No overarching narrative, no likable protagonist, no actual purpose. It's neither fiction nor non-fiction. Not poetry nor prose. It cites no sources, names no characters. It offends for sport.

Its tone alternates erratically. Its attempts at humor frequently fall flat. Its attempts at insight lack falsifiability. It fails to explore the person, "me," behind scores of baseless assertions. It is hostile to you, the reader, you misguided fuck.

All of which, of course, *begs* the question, *why, then, should you care?*

Well. You shouldn't. Read something else. Do something else! You take care now! Byyyeeee!

The truth is I'm embarrassed by this. Because, for one, it is highly presumptuous to think anyone would care to hear the private thoughts of an irrelevant stranger. Second, much of this is in poor taste, is incriminating, or makes me look bad.

So really, move right along. Best wishes. Fare thee well. Get ye gone. All the best. Toodaloo! It does mean the world to me that you remotely considered purchasing this pure work of art to keep atop your toilet tank to confuse your guests 11 minutes at a time as they take a

> Shit, I spent an embarrassingly large amount of time on this.

Classified

IF YOU'LL believe it, my parents met in the late 1970s... online.

Well, as close to *online* as you could get back then. They met through the personal ads section of a newspaper. The paper was "India Abroad" which was the fresh-off-the-Gujurati-boat Tinder of its time.

"Mustachioed Engineer Seeks Bombshell Babe" is what I assume my dad's ad read. He has always been judicious with words. My mom, a free-spirited painter from Delhi, swiped right!

...on the rotary phone. And the rest was, as they say...

Arranged! For their second date, they went to a wedding.

Their own!

My parents are what one might call "too cool." They went to Burning Man. Without me. They go on ten-day silent Vipassana retreats. Like it was Pilates class. They lived with a Peruvian family for three months in their sixties trying to learn Spanish.

They have the paragon of marriage: best friends, explorers; committed and equal partners. My sibling-free childhood in the suburbs of San Francisco and Vancouver, BC was, in a word, idyllic.

Which is to disclaim that the words in this book have been entirely uninspired by strife.

And to brag that I am the product of an engineer and an artist.

Belated Introduction

I DON'T KNOW what this book is, let alone what it is about.

I do know it's an edited transcription of things that crossed my mind from the ages of 28 to 33, which happened to be the calendar years of 2015-2020; I took the duration of the pandemic's quarantine to polish it, and, at the now ancient age of 35, in mid-2021, I'm publishing it as this book.

The passages in this book are aspirationally *bits* but I misnome them *essays*. All have some version of a punchline, but conveniently, my definition of punchline includes provoking thought and not having a punchline.

I will say that much of this originated from ideas I had for comedy bits during my one-time hobby of performing stand-up comedy at open mics in New York City. I did some 150 of those. I never got particularly great at performing stand-up—the nervous energy I exude does not elicit laughter—but I did enjoy doing it, presumably in the same way that some people enjoy self-harm.

I tried to do new material each time, once or twice a week, which forced me to begin a fierce writing habit, largely during long subway rides, typed in Gmail drafts. I did increasingly fewer open mics and spent increasingly more nights alone writing. At some point, I migrated the scattered email drafts to Word, resulting in a wildly disorganized jumble of incomplete sentences, long-winded rants, and the occasional punchline.

But one day, reading that mess of words, a meta-thought occurred to me. *Maybe I could turn this into a book.* Then, I did that; this.

> One other way I would love to see this book used is as a party game. One person opens a page at random and reads the passage on it, and everyone discusses. Come on, that would be so much more fun than charades.

Sales Projections

Will this book sit atop the NYT bestselling list for *years*? Will it usher in a new cultural era leading me to be labeled *The Millennial Mark Twain*? Will it be translated into 36 languages, uniting the world, bringing levity to dark topics, giving clarity of purpose to the masses? Yes, I am elated to say, *it will!!*

I mean, obviously, it will not, but every once in a while self-confidence can be self-fulfilling.

In practice, whether it does get a large readership or not is up to you alone: Will you share passages from this book in conversation and on social media? Will you stick it on your "top 100 books I read this year" list, you unequivocally pretentious prick? If you, on average, do, then the power of exponentiation will take it from there, and we'll have a shot at changing the world. If you, on average, do not, then these pages shall remain the obscure words of a madman.

I wish you well in this choose-your-own-adventure.

INTRODUCTION

> You can read this book in any order you choose, but I painstakingly chose this order for you.

> My weird flex is that I don't watch TV, sports, or movies. I barely read, and I deplore novels. "What do you do with your time?" Well, I wrote this book.

Story Junkie

I FIND IT KIND of annoying that people like stories so much. Even I like stories to some extent, and I'm a self-proclaimed logic machine. When I first shared these essays with a few friends, everyone said, "I like the parts where you tell a story about yourself!"

Of course that's what you like, you predictable natural automaton. Because you can't handle the cold, hard truths of the kind I would prefer to be spitting at you. So, we'll compromise. I'll sneak the points I want to make into semi-stories. Like this one.

> Forewords are dumb. Just start the damned book.

> In writing, I value concision and precision.

My chapter names are all words I made up.

My acts have spice levels.

Just because.

I have fast-recited many of these essays on TikTok, @niktalksfast.

The first half of this book is grand misdirection to trick you into reading the second half of the book, which you would never buy if it were a separate book, as many suggested I should make it.

I am the rare combination of self-effacing and egomaniacal. You'll see.

I ask you to judge this book not as a book but as a work of art. As the inaugural work in a new form of art which is expressing the totality of one irrelevant person's out-of-the-mainstream thoughts.

> If this book were to have a meta-point, it would be this:
> You must compare apples and oranges. Anything less is criminal.

> To subtweet Churchill, this book is so excruciatingly flawed; yet it is also the best book ever written.

Quick Plug: UrRong.com

I made a website for this book, www.urrong.com, and I put some of these essay on there such that you can filter them in various ways, misguidedly tell me imrong, and invite others to tell you *ur*rong about whatever ideas you would like to contribute to the global conversation.

Will this website become the next major blogging platform? I am elated to say it will.

I also made a bunch of TikTok videos of me speed reciting these essays and have embedded them into my essays' pages on UrRong, as you can do as well.

Just to be a dick, I'm going to remind you to check out UrRong on every subsequent page.

Act I:
Bell Pepper:
Social Situations

being a pansy in the dating game

FLEURTATION

Snitches of the Soul

SOMETIMES, I'LL develop a secret crush on an acquaintance of mine. I'll be hanging out with her, talking to her, thinking, *Goddamn it, this chick is the best. She's amusingly awkward, sexy like a librarian, so incredibly creative. The two of us could be the quirky analogue of a power coup...*

Then I'll notice that she, herself, is giving me a quizzical look.

"Why are you looking at me like that?" she wants to know.

Before I can muster an alibi for my gaze, I'll remember, *Shit. I forgot that my eyes are a bunch of little snitches. I was trying to keep this little affection on the down-low, but these rats took it upon themselves to become informants, yelling, "He likes you! He likes you!! We also greatly enjoy relaying processing the image of your face!"*

You better watch yourself, eyes. Because snitches get stitches. Betray me again and I *will* sew you shut.

And, Scene

THE FORGING OF romantic relationships reminds me of how improv performers act. You're constantly guessing what your partner means by what they said, what they want you to do, whether, realistically, this would be a good place to end it.

Misunderstandings get blown out of proportion, and as you're about to deliver the closer you planned from the start, someone taps you on your shoulder and takes your place in what was about to be the perfect scene.

But I'm a Creep

Being creepy is, in my experience, just an asymmetry of attraction. If one person's attraction to another is conspicuous and inspires unease, that's creepy, perhaps by definition. But if both parties have such great mutual admiration that they become socially inept in each other's presence... well, that's the beautiful thing we call love.

I'll admit that if I'm hanging with a woman I have genuine affection for, I will become textbook creepy.

I'll gaze into her eyes when she's not looking and then avert eye contact when she does. I'll fail to carry my weight in conversation; I'll mumble something accidentally inappropriate nonetheless. My body language would make even the blind uneasy.

Which is to say that if you're on a date with me, and I'm being remarkably charming, engaging you in clever, intellectual, flirtatious banter, and you're having a wonderful time, then you should end the date right there. Because, it means, I'm just not that into you.

> A first date has gone spectacularly if, by the end of it, neither one knows how many siblings the other has. This is one of many inside jokes I have with myself, so never mind if you don't get it.

Pick-Up Line

I don't use dating apps, but I still manage to get dates the old-fashioned way: meeting a woman circumstantially, asking for her number, and arranging to meet up later.

A friend remarked to me that women these days must be so used to men not doing that, that they give up their number out of pure confusion. Which might be true.

"Why yes, I DO come here often!" they figuratively gush. "What a unique and thoughtful question! Here my digits."

Fast Forward

Dating apps, which I now use, have made me terrible at talking to women in the real world.

Now, I'll look at a woman across the room whom I'd like nothing more than to get to know as a person, and mentally flick them one way or the other.

And that will conclude my pick-up effort.

What a sad state of affairs.

Loquacious

I WENT ON A SECOND DATE that was scheduled to last two days straight. We hit it off at a blackjack table in Atlantic City and arranged to meet back at the casino hotel some weeks later for a weekend together. She was a divorced mother of teenagers from the Philly suburbs. I was a 30-year-old struggling entrepreneur from exploiting cheap weekday casino room rates to Airbnb my apartment.

So, we began our double-day date, and she did most of the talking, as is typical with me on dates and with me in general. I don't talk much, and I will encourage others to carry the conversation to the extent that they are willing.

But on day two of this weekend getaway, somehow, we got on the topic of the nature of existence. I probably brought it up, as sometimes I do. She followed up my remark with a question, then another. I guess I got too excited, because, on a wild whim, fueled by liquid courage, I proposed...

...that she hear my theory on the origin of consciousness. And she said yes!

So, I delivered my convoluted theory about how consciousness came into being, starting with the initial spark of life and ending with our ability to have this conversation on this hotel room bed at all. There was a lot to cover, so it took me a good twenty minutes to get through.

She listened intently, and when I concluded my theory, she summarized what she learned, "So that's how I get you to start talking! I ask you about existential stuff!"

Imaginary Girlfriend

Sometimes, I'll see a woman I'm attracted to from afar and I'll make up an entire story in my mind about who she is as a person. She studied art history at Yale and did Teach for America! She is exceedingly compassionate yet bitingly sarcastic! The maximum volume on her voice is awkwardly quiet like mine!

In reality, she might be the worst, the opposite of my type. She might be mainstream, dense, and shallow. Self-congratulatory, superstitious, temperamental.

But so long as I never introduce myself, the dream of who she is—of who we could be together—can stay decidedly alive.

being a social animal while antisocial

ANTISOCIALIZING

> When I'm in public, sometimes I'll make eye contact with a stranger. They'll look away, as will I. But then I'll look back to see if they looked back too. *Because, if they did,* I'll think, *maybe they saw something in me.*

Passing Strangers

You know one thing we haven't figured out as a society?

It's what the proper etiquette is when you're walking behind a person who is walking a bit slower than you are.

If nothing changes velocity-wise, you're on a collision course to awkwardness, and everyone knows it. There will be a brief but seemingly eternal moment during which you and they walk together in unison, side by side, avoiding acknowledgment if all goes as planned. There's something about that prospect that makes me, and I think everyone, so uncomfortable.

So, what's a man to do? As I've worked it out, a man has got two options: slow down or speed up.

Slowing down is fine but imperfect; you will have conceded your ideal pace of locomotion to that of a stranger. And what does that say about you if you are willing to capitulate so easily?

But speeding up is even more fraught. Because to overtake the person you'll need to accelerate *significantly*, so as to not only pass them but to also gain real distance on them. Otherwise, the roles merely reverse with them tailgating your buttocks.

So, fine. You accelerate hard. You leave them many meters behind. But I must report that your dilemma is not yet over. For if you slow down to your original pace, you may inflict upon them the shame of knowing that you unnaturally picked up your pace to avoid that innocent moment of togetherness you both could have shared on a block you probably both frequent, in a city you probably both call home.

Retraction

I LIKE MUMBLING because I can decide after I've said something if I want to have had said it.

Me: [mumbles]

Her: What did you say?

Me: *Contemplates wisdom of having said that*

Me: Huh? Nothing. Don't worry about it.

Her: Nikhil, what the hell did you just say to me?

Me: Never *mind*!

Her: Sounds like you had something to say!

Me: Well, I retract it!

Cleanliness

I THINK PEOPLE'S cleanliness standards are way too high. It pisses me off when I go to someone's place and they give some pained speech before opening their door, foreshadowing chaos within, "I am *so* sorry. It is *so* messy in here. I didn't have time to clean. Oh my God, I'm just *so* embarrassed to let you see the filth in which I reside!"

And then, after assuring them of my supreme nonjudgmentalness on this matter, we go in, and everything is basically spotless, except that a couple of couch pillows are askew and there's a magazine open with earrings lying on top.

I'll think, *fuck you and your cleanliness standards.*

My apartment, as *I* would define it, is *a little bit messy.* I have dried urine on the bathroom floor. There is a three-day-old bowl of beans calcifying on my desk. A mandarin orange peel coexisting with an undershirt in the kitchen. Pen caps, empty water bottles, dried spinach leaves, fruit flies, stuff—*just stuff!* — everywhere! That's me on a good day.

But I don't see the mess I live in as foul. In fact, I don't see it at all. Maybe it is an undiagnosed neurological disorder. Maybe it's the purest form of apathy. But when I look at the objective filth in which I live, I see normalcy, not mess.

There was *one* time when I saw my apartment as everyone else does, and it was wild. A friend and I had taken acid on Halloween night. I got home at four in the morning, still tripping, and per usual, it was the scene of a tornado-ravaged dwelling. Cutlery on the floor, nail clippings on the counter, the works! But somehow, in that hallucinogenic state, I saw the mess through the eyes of respectable members of society. I saw it as the unspeakably squalid living quarters that it truly was. I thought, *what the fuck is this? Are you kidding me, Nikhil? Who lives like this? This is disgusting—maybe even a sanitation hazard. No wonder no one dates you. You are going to clean all this up and treat the habit of tidying up as an integral part of the adult life you profess to lead! Tomorrow!*

Exhausted, I fell asleep and woke up at 2PM, frazzled, still wearing the remains of the Catholic nun costume whose irony I mistakenly thought would be clever. I looked around and saw the same mess I had seen the night before. And I thought, *this seems normal.* Despite my very best efforts, and trust me I tried, I could not for the life of me find it off-putting.

And I never had that experience again.

One-Sided

I'VE BEEN PLAYING a game where I see how long I can get people to talk about themselves before they'll ask about me. The current high score is ~~forty-two minutes.~~

Update: one hour and twelve minutes.

Human Resources

YOU KNOW THE EXPRESSION, "friends with benefits?" I think it's funny how jobs are also said to come "with benefits."

I like to imagine myself starting a new job and, as the first group orientation session is wrapping up, and the orientation leader opens it up to Q&A, I'd pipe in with, "So, I understand this is a job with benefits…"

I would pause, then say suggestively, "dot, dot, dot…" in case they didn't hear my sexy ellipses.

Send It Back

YOU KNOW HOW you can tell if someone has money? Like, *real money*? They'll send stuff back at restaurants—fast-food chains and Michelin-starred eateries alike. Fries insufficiently fried at Wendy's? Send it back. Foie gras insufficiently gras at Pierre's? Send it back.

He who comes from a modest background will remove the human hair from his angel hair without incident. But she whose family vacations in Seychelles will have her melting ice cream re-scooped twice.

> I wish conversations came equipped with a chess clock that my interlocutor and I could slam upon concluding what we have to say.

Opinion Irrelevance

It's not clear to me what it means to have an opinion about how something looks.

Let's say someone asks me, "How do you like my haircut?" What do I say? I can say it bears similarity to the haircuts people of your age and income tend to sport, and therefore is suitable to who you are. Do I like it? I don't know how to access the part of my brain that forms preferences.

Even if I could, what are you hoping to gain? Insight into the entire population's perspective from me, a single, unreliable data point?

Don't ask me if your shoes go with your outfit. Don't ask me if your suit complements your eyes. I don't know, and if I did, you shouldn't care.

Talk Faster

I'm shocked how slowly people talk. Whenever I'm watching a talk on YouTube or listening to an audiobook, I make the speed 2x just so I can bear to listen to it. I know there are other people like me but why are we the ones who have to change the speed from the default?

Going forward I'm going to talk as fast as I wish people would and if you've got a problem with that, you can go ahead and modify my speed to 50%.

> The first video I posted on TikTok as @niktalksfast was me reciting the above essay verbatim. It got over a million views, which blew my mind and further inflated my ego.

Stereotype A

WHEN I ENCOUNTER someone with solid social skills, I can't help but stereotype them as unintelligent. I realize that this is factually inaccurate and mean-spirited of me to say. But I'll keep digging nonetheless.

If you're extraordinarily smart, you must spend so much time and energy listening to yourself think and read that what's left of the cognitive capacity you have to offer others amounts to mere table scraps of geniality. Conversely, if you spend little time being lost in thought, assessing incongruencies, then you'll have all the spare mental capacity in the world to observe how people interact, mimic the successful among them, and become incredibly personable along the way. *This* is the bigotry I lay claim to.

Yes, I know this is a hurtful stereotype directed at a group of people that has within it brilliant members. Yes, I'm broadly affixing the labels of "dumb," "poorly read," and "social imitator" to the celebrated community of well-spoken, affable socialites.

But, fuck it. *Someone's* gotta pick on the cool kids.

the tragic comedy of being broken up with

UNREQUITIA

Brasierrrrr

I HIRED a cleaning lady because my apartment had seen better days. She was going through my closet and found a bra in there. She made some good-natured joke about it and put it aside. It was the property of a woman with whom I had been engaging in relations on a roughly weekly basis.

So, that weekend, the bra's owner came over late at night and as she was packing up to leave the next morning, I said, "Oh, by the way, you left your bra here last time."

"I did?"

"Yeah." I fetched it and handed it to her.

Oh god, the look on her face.

"That's not my bra!!" She threw it back at my head.

Now, listen. It's not unheard of for me to be a two-timing son-of-a-bitch if relations are just casual, as were these. But in this *particular instance*, I totally wasn't. I just hadn't cleaned out my closet in such a long time that a bra remained from a former fling who had moved to Eastern Europe six months prior.

I explained how the bra's occupant had been out of this hemisphere for over a demi-year and how it had been even longer than that since I cleaned my filthy closet. Somehow, that didn't help my case.

And the once-a-week thing became a once-a-month thing, then a never-again thing. Sometimes you just can't recover from a dating flub.

> Incidentally, If you're a 34C, I have a gently used bra free to a good home.

Would You Rather

I quite dislike hypothetical questions. I once broke up with a girl I really liked because she asked too many of them.

"One more, one more!" she said. "Would you rather be a blind elephant or a deaf cat?"

"I'll tell you what I'd rather," I said, "I'd rather we not see each other anymore."

Retraction

In that last story, I misrepresented the truth. She broke up with me.

And then I cried for days.

Here, incidentally, how that specific breakup went down:

> A girl I was dating was feeling down one day. I meant to ask, "What's wrong?" but what came out was, "What's wrong with you?"
> She broke up with me on the spot.

Personals

I expect the following personal ad to be valid for the rest of my life:

```
Single Indian male seeks human female for three-month
romantic relationship followed by six-year weird
friendship.
```

Ex-Girlfriends

I'M FRIENDS with my ex-girlfriends and some people find that weird. But here's the thing: I don't see them as ex-girlfriends; I see them as alumnae.

They gained admission, they went through the program, and graduation was bittersweet.

So, later this year, I'm going to give them all a call.

"Hey Sarah," I'll say. "Listen. I'm actually raising funds for a prospective candidate who doesn't have the financial means to support me, and I was wondering if you'd considering making a kind donation."

...

...

...

"...Hello... Sarah?"

Dark at night

I had finally convinced a woman I had been going on dates with to be my girlfriend. We decided to meet up on Saturday morning for our very first date as an NYC couple: a day trip to the beach at Coney Island. It promised to be super cute.

Anyway, the Friday night before our trip, I decided to stay in for a night of smoking up, thinking, writing, and browsing Wikipedia—my actual idea of an ideal Friday night.

Anyway, as part of this particular Friday-night mental expedition, I realized an embarrassing intellectual blind spot of mine: I didn't know why it gets hot in the summer. *Does it have to do with how far Earth is in its orbit from the Sun?* That seemed wrong because when it's winter here, it's summer in Australia. I must have been truant the day my third-grade teacher taught this.

So, I Googled it. I learned, at the advanced age of 27, that seasons are caused by the tilt of the Earth relative to the Sun. On a given patch of land, more tilt away from the sun means the same number of heat-causing radiation-carrying photons get dispersed across a slightly larger surface area, delivering less heat to each square inch; hence, seasons. *Oh.* That made sense. But I did feel silly for not having known it earlier.

Anyway, the next morning, my new girlfriend (!) and I found our ways to the W. 4th St. station, where we had coordinated meeting to transfer to the F train. I experienced the emotion of giddiness.

Anyway, at one point during a lull in our subway, I attempted to demonstrate vulnerability by confessing that I had to look up the literal reason for the seasons. I humored her by sharing the thing about the photon dispersement on the wild chance she also didn't know.

Our conversation meandered to the topic of planetary movements. I attempted a joke. "Well, unless you stop and think about it, it's almost easy to forget why it gets dark at night!"

She paused for a moment and with the most breathtaking deadpan delivery I have seen, she quipped, "Wait, why *does* it get dark at night?"

She was obviously joking, so I laughed, unable to maintain the deadpan banter.

But then I realized she wasn't joking.

So, we, um, talked about it. She had, I guess, forgotten that Earth turns all the way around relative to the sun every single day and that the length of a day is defined as the arbitrary duration it takes Earth to do that.

Fine. *So what?* My girlfriend didn't know why it gets dark at night. I didn't know why it gets hot in the summer! *Same diff, right??*

It was too late. My laugh at her expense conveyed to her that I did not think it was the *same diff*. Implicit in that being that *I thought I was better than her.*

We moved on from the topic, but we both felt a tension had been introduced.

The beach was nice when we arrived. We soaked in some sun. Applied sunscreen to each others. She waded in the water. I made a deformed castle.

We held hands, as couples do. We displayed affection publicly as lusting young people do. We got ice cream in waffle cones, as beachgoers do.

The motions were all there, but something was still amiss. Could we get past the dark-at-night thing? We dared not speak of it, but it remained the cloud on this photon-dense day.

As the sun drifted westward, we washed the sand from our toes and left the beach in the late afternoon

After a long, oddly silent subway ride back to Manhattan, we exited the train at W. 4th where we could transfer to one of our places. She suggested we get out of the station and go for a walk instead.

She seemed tense. Now more so than before.

We pushed the turnstiles and made our way through a meandering alleyway of the West Village. We made small talk about the weather and our surroundings.

She grabbed a sidewalk tree and stopped walking. She looked down, then at me, then down again. A tear rolled down her face. She said that she has been thinking. About this. About us. That she has really enjoyed getting to know me.

That maybe we're too different as people. That she had fun today. That she hopes we can stay in touch as friends.

We embraced, exchanged pleasantries, and as parted ways as exes.

Alas, there was no other way.

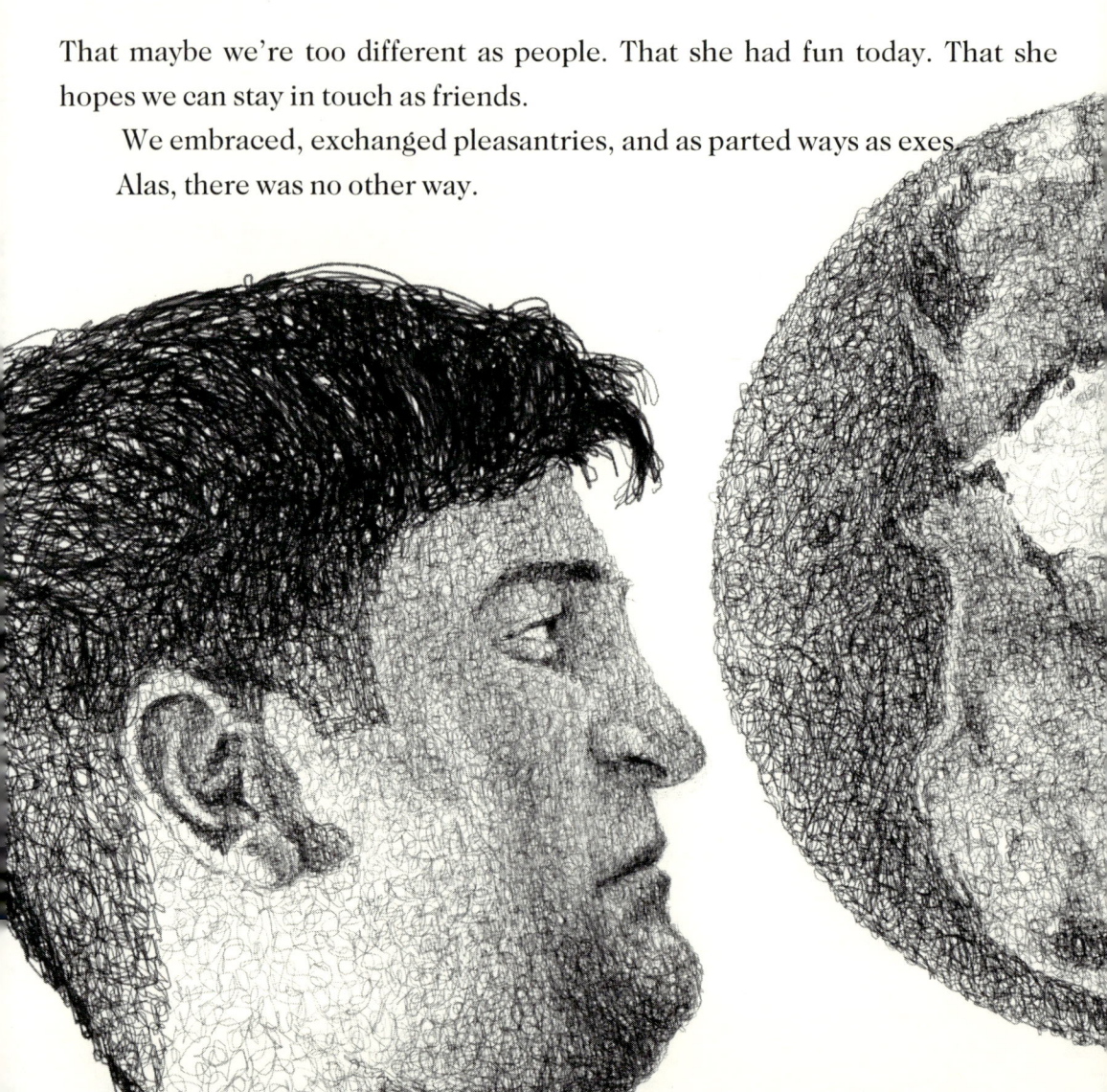

the person we become online

HOMO SWIPIAN

Texting

The internet, especially messaging and social apps, is a weird phenomenon in that it fulfills some, at times all, of your basic social needs as a person. There have been entire days where I didn't use my vocal cords to communicate with another person once; yet, I ended the day socially drained from a full twelve hours of relentless socializing online.

> "Came here to say exactly that!" is the most annoying comment that litters the Internet.

Internet Stalkers

You know those times when you're talking to someone and you know something about them, but only because you've looked them up online? You can't really reference that you know this thing about them, because then you'll have to have a whole conversation about looking people up on the Internet, and this totally reasonable practice will invariably be referred to as *stalking*.

Best not to open that can of worms.

> Talk is cheap. But texting doesn't even require eye contact.

Browser Clutter

I usually have 80-130 tabs open in my web browser.

What if I need to re-reference something??? is the thought.
This is my pitch for *Hoarders: Google Chrome Edition.*

LinkedIn Congrats

LinkedIn is always telling me to congratulate people. Maia got a new job? *Say congrats!* Preeti got canned? *Say congrats!* Marco stuck around at the same dead-end job for five whole years? *OMG, congrats!*

Honestly, I wouldn't be surprised to see LinkedIn nudging me to grieve the untimely death of a former coworker.

Samuel has updated his living status. Say congrats!

Uber Drivers

Uber drivers seem scared of you.

"Is the music okay? How about the temperature? Is your day going satisfactorily? May I offer you this gift of homemade baklava? Would you prefer it if I drove with one hand and massaged your feet with the other?"

I miss the days of crass, misogynistic, don't-give-a-fuck cabbies. A certain edge, gone.

Aspiration

You ever see someone successful in a way that you want to be, and think to yourself, *goddamn it, is there any chance that I'll be that successful when I'm their age?*

The next logical step in that thought process, at least for me, is to find them on LinkedIn or Wikipedia, reverse engineer the calendar year that they would have been my age, and see how their life, then, compares to mine, now. Sure, sometimes, by my age, they had already made it as a member of the big leagues, and I'll become disheartened. But more often than not, they had some desk job! They were in some supporting role! They were, like me, unknown and obscure!! That gives me hope that maybe there's still time to be great.

> I know I shouldn't do that—compare myself to others and obsess about achieving some nebulous notion of success. But I figured I'd admit that this is something I do. Wow, it felt good to get that off my chest.

Unsubscribe

As I'm sure you do too, I get a lot of newsletters, updates, and solicitations over email from companies to whom I may or may or not have given my email address. Fortunately, there is now a law that requires companies to include an unsubscribe link in such emails. So, I spend eight minutes every morning unsubscribing from such emails, mistaking that for productivity.

I also get emails and texts from people I know; friends, I might call them. Julio sent me a link to an article that I guess I'm supposed to reply to with an opinion. Nina told me about what a dick her date last night was, to which I am required to offer sympathy. But, sometimes, I don't give a shit. But I don't want to confront them. Here's what I propose to the FCC: it should be requisite for unsolicited social correspondence to come with an unsubscribe link. You're rambling about your inconsiderate coworker? Unsubscribe. You found the cutest cat video I must watch? Unsubscribe. You just said "hey" and expect a reply? Unsubscribe!!

Listen Carefully

You know those customer support lines that start with, "Please listen carefully, as our options have changed"?

What the fuck do they think we do with our time? Memorize the sequence of digits to get to their gardening department's delivery service's hours of operations on Tuesday in English?

That's as absurd as if your romantic partner started some argument with, "Please listen carefully, as the source of my anger has changed."

It's like, bitch, I don't remember which of your buttons I pressed last time. Just tell me what I've got to do this time to keep your monologue as short as possible.

Social Anxiety

Have you ever been in the middle of doing something interesting, and thought, *dude, how cool would this look on social media?*

Sometimes that question is genuine; you're actually not sure.

But other times, it is rhetorical. Of course, that would look cool on social media.

But it is probably also true that capturing that moment and posting it to social media will disrupt the wholesomeness of the moment you seek to capture. At that point, you must take a stance: Should you reduce your enjoyment to look cool on social media? Or should you take in the moment for what it is?

That, I think, is one of life's great questions.

Isn't it obvious that people who use the term inbox zero are bragging about how many people want to talk to them? I'm a struggling entrepreneur; no one reaches out to me unless I spam them with un-solicitations. Inbox zero is effortless on my part and that couldn't be any less of a flex.

growing old with family

SENESCENTION

Only Child

As an only child, I find the term "only child" subtly disparaging. Why can't we be the normal ones and have you sibling-folk get dubbed "also children"? As in, "Bob fears peer disapproval and lacks identity because he's a feckless, maladjusted also child."

> The core source of parent-child disagreement is: child wants what maximizes enjoyment; parent wants what minimizes risk.

Sex-Ed

I remember how I learned about sex. I must have been 7 or 8. We had one of those old-time encyclopedia sets at home where there are 16 books filled with just... encyclopedia stuff. So, I directed my hand about three quarters down the shelf and picked up the Rhinoceros—Uterus volume, in search of the entry on "sex." It was a word I had heard before but only in the context of it being something people didn't want to talk about around me. Within some 25 seconds, my mouth was agape, and I felt truly guilty for possessing this forbidden knowledge.

> Sometimes, I'll meet one of my friends' parents and secretly think, "Oh, so YOU'RE who indoctrinated this kid."

Second-Hand Accent

I WAS BORN in America to Indian parents. They speak English well; my mom even used to teach ESL. But they have accents, as immigrants do, and every once in a while, I'll learn that my whole life I've been pronouncing certain words incorrectly. I was taking a photography class that involved the use of a darkroom, and I mentioned to a friend that I need to DEV-a-LUP the shots I took. My friend said with genuine confusion, "You need to what? You mean develop?"

> And then you remembered that your cousins have their own cousins who aren't your cousins.

Virtuosic Typing

I remember being young and seeing my mom typing for her job. I would think, *oh my goodness that is such an amazing skill.* It seemed right up there with the abilities of concert pianists. That you could have a thought and effortlessly convert it into the exact muscle twitches that make your fingers tap just the right buttons—five or more per second! —in just the right order! —was truly mind-boggling to me.

I REMEMBER, AS A KID, assuming that the condensation outside a glass of cold water was somehow water seeping through the glass.

Childhood, on VHS

I went to visit my parents, and while they usually bust out some family photos to reminisce, this time, they announced that they had converted old VHS tapes to DVD so that we could watch them.

It was so uncomfortable to watch. In part because I was, in these videos, roughly as mature as a kid would be for that age. But it's me, and I'm watching myself be a moronic two-year-old, an uninformed eight-year-old, a painfully awkward thirteen-year-old.

What's more, I was reminded of how I got to be who I am and how many of the mannerisms I had when I was a young child I still have as an adult.

Rich Dad, Present Dad

It is said that some wealthy parents offer their children money but not love and those children grow up with a void that no amount of money can replace. The reason, I suggest, that such parents neglect their kids is that the opportunity cost of spending time with their children is simply too high.

An hour of making faces at your precocious two-year-old? That might cost a middle-class parent some $60 of lost overtime, a small price to pay for priceless moments. But that same hour might amount to $20,000 of foregone capital gains for some mega-rich hedge fund manager. I'm pretty sure nobody loves their kid *that* much.

Encouraging Idiocy

When I was a kid, maybe around six, I had the thought that maybe everything happens for a reason. I told that to my mom and she was stunned that a child would have such insight. When I was in the fourth grade, I came up with a scheme that would surely produce perpetual motion. It used gears to create increasingly fast circular momentum which would power a generator that would power the original gear. My dad, an engineer, was surprised at the ingenuity and encouraged me to pursue it.

But obviously, things do not happen for a reason; what would that even mean to be true? Preordainment is not a thing. And obviously, the very first law of thermodynamics prohibits my scheme. Perpetual motion is right up there with alchemy in terms of desirable but impossible feats.

I wish someone had corrected me then instead of encouraging my idiocy so that I could have steered my thinking in the right direction.

Growin' Up

How do you feel about how you've grown up in the eyes of your family? They had expectations, guesses, or hopes of who you might become. Now you're of the age they once speculated about. How did you disappoint them? How did you surprise them? When exactly was it that you decided to be who you ended up being?

Deadline

When you reach a certain age, you can't be creative anymore. Eventually, you just have too much information in your head, too many competing priorities, too many individuals to remain aware of. There simply does not remain the cognitive capacity and open space to have new, original ideas.

> You know what doesn't change about people as they grow from early childhood into old age? Their smile.

Breakup Advocacy

Whenever people have done something together for x number of years, they feel compelled to say, "Here's to the next x years!" Like, "Aw, we've been married for 15 years, here's to the next 15, baby!"

But what's with the expectation to renew relationship contracts into the distant future? Why always double the duration of the relationship to date? I'd like to be able to say, "Nice! We've been best friends since we met ten years ago! I'd like to make a toast! Here's to now being *as good a time as any* to begin growing apart. Because if you and I had met today, there's very little chance we would go out of our way to become even passing acquaintances."

Life in an Evening

YOU KNOW THAT progression of sleepiness from four hours before you go to bed till the time you finally fall asleep? I feel like the aging process can be described similarly but spread out over, say, 80 years.

During the first of those four hours before you fall asleep, representing the first 20 years of life, the night is young. You're productive, curious, soaking in information. Sleep is but a vague, distant, theoretical concept.

In the second hour, ages 20 to 40, you check your watch. "Oh, would you look at the time?" You're still firing away, getting work done, spending quality time with your family, but time is going by faster than you expected. Now, at least, sleep is on your radar.

In the third hour, representing ages 40 to 60, you're now generally tired, not that you're intending to slow down or anything. But things that were easy an hour ago seem to require a fair bit more concentration. "Honey, I'm going to go lie down," you announce.

The last hour before bed, 60 to 80: now you're exhausted. You try to pursue a new endeavor but fail. It's probably time for sleep soon. You say goodnight to your loved ones, you get a few things in order, and then you fall asleep.

At this point in both sides of the analogy, the jury is out as to what exactly happens next.

achieving greatness

PINNACLASCENTION

Entitlement

ENTITLEMENT IS A THING that gets frowned upon. Entitlement is the internalized belief that says, *Yes, this is owed to me. Yes, I am deserving of that.* But the idea that you are owed something by society is a pretense that is rightfully scorned. You aren't owed shit.

I have to say, though, that *having* a sense of entitlement appears to be a handy skill to have, its dubious social acceptability notwithstanding.

———

Today, a friend asked me if I thought college was a valuable experience. I responded, "I think what was valuable was the sense of entitlement I developed." Saying that aloud startled me. I couldn't possibly mean that. Could I?

———

Once upon a time, I was a shy teenager who had lived a simple life in the suburbs of San Francisco and Vancouver. I went to NYU my freshman year, then transferred to Penn; I was in the Stern and Wharton undergraduate business. I would later also get into Y Combinator, a noted startup accelerator.

I worked quite intensely to get into and through these programs. I had taken on a lot of debt. And there I was claiming my chief extraction from all that toil and tuition was... a *sense of entitlement?*

I have come to conclude that, *yes, this is my true stance.* Entitlement is ultimately why my alma maters mattered.

The point of business schools, I now believe, is to take in timid nerds like the one-time me and churn out entitled brats like my present-day self.

Here's a magic trick. Pick any elite business school you can think of. Go to their website. Find the tagline they use to pitch themselves. Let me guess: it *screams* entitlement. Here, for your reference, are the taglines of Stanford's, Penn's, and Harvard's business schools, respectively:

"CHANGE LIVES. CHANGE ORGANIZATIONS. CHANGE THE WORLD."

"INCUBATING IDEAS. DRIVING INSIGHTS. CREATING LEADERS."

"WE EDUCATE LEADERS WHO MAKE A DIFFERENCE IN THE WORLD."

How do you lead? How do you make a difference? How do you change the world?

Maybe it starts with believing you can.

Who in their right mind believes they, a single schmuck, can bend the future to the one they envision, can inspire legions of disciples to acquiesce to their demands.

Entitled people, that's who. People who expect greatness to fall in their laps and whine about it if it does not.

Business schools' dog-whistle taglines whisper unto their prospective applicants, *Hey you, aspiring corporate ascender: chill in our walled gardens for just a hot sec, and we'll spit you out with straight delusions of grandeur, son! Heyyy, nerdy mathlete! It would be our honor to strip you of your adorbs humility and make you see humanity as the predictable, manipulable peons that they are!*

All this talk of being the most boss you can reminds me of a Notoriously voluminous businessman's hit single, "Get Money." Its hook goes like this, *fuck bitches; get money*, a meditative chant repeated again and again to great effect.

Because, hey, if business schools' taglines were just a teensy, weensy bit more transparent, that's exactly the line they'd be updated to.

Sample Bias

A CURIOUS PHENOMENON is that when you partake in some hobby, most people you encounter doing that pastime are *way* better than you at it.

Think about it. At yoga class, everyone else sails through boat pose. At the tennis courts, everyone's overhead smashes yours. At the poker table, you're the royal fish.

Why? Well, people who do something more frequently are more commonly doing it. So, they make up a disproportionate fraction of the people doing that activity at any given time. If practice makes perfect and practice involves showing up, then those who've shown up are more probably perfect.

Notoriety

THE IDEA OF having to apologize to the public is very appealing to me. Because that means you've "made it" to the extent that the society, at large, demands from you the genuine expression of remorse as token rectification for the vast scale of offense you have caused.

That kind of fame—that sounds sick, actually.

Misdeeds

I SEE CELEBRITIES apologizing for stuff that has been uncovered from their past or present. Some stuff, like sexual assault, is inexcusable, and there is no defense.

But for everything else—the resurfaced tweets, the marital infidelity, the pilfering of coffers—their response, instead of contrition, should be this: "Look, we all try to get away with stuff that we're confident we won't get caught having done. You do it. I did it. And I decline to say if I continue to do it. The difference is that people care enough about me to expose my prior misdeeds."

So, when some cyclist is caught doping or a CEO is exposed to have cooked the books, they shouldn't suppose the public will buy their denial or accept their apology. They should say, sheepishly, "I didn't think I'd get caught."

And then hope that the world can relate.

I, for one, notice my moral compass going south the moment I'm sure no one will ever find out what I've done. If that's not relatable, oops.

> I'd like to start a sperm bank for the most intellectually gifted sperm donors, but only because I came up with a sweet name for it: Summa Cum Laude.

Sum Ting Wong

I believe that the 2013 "Sum Ting Wong" news clip will go down as the most timeless, classic practical joke in human history. We'll laugh about it with our grandkids, and they'll do the same with theirs. Future civilizations will study it alongside the Pyramids of Giza, the concertos of Mozart and the theory of general relativity as being among the most significant of human achievements.

If you don't know what I'm talking about, I feel bad for you, son. But look it up on YouTube it and witness some rogue intern's historic feat of misdirection.

Ascetic

I PRESENT TO YOU my *I'm Better Than You* diet: no meat, no movies, no spouse, no TV, no car, no bike, no fish, no faith, no sports, no eggs, no religion, no dairy, no kids. I should probably get a bike.

> Some have suggested I may be "on the spectrum." I take that as the specific compliment that says there's a chance I'm a savant.

Star

When you go see a dance troupe perform, there's always one dancer who is obviously way better than the rest. Isolated movements. Impeccable timing. Personality oozing. The works.

I wonder if she feels pressure to tone it down, to pretend she's no better than the rest. She shouldn't, of course. She's wonderful, a true joy to watch. But I have to assume there's something about being conspicuously more talented than your peers that is a little embarrassing to have to flaunt.

> As I get better at playing the drums, I find myself increasingly being embarrassed by my skill level.

> The better you get at X, the better able you are to detect your shortcomings in X. So, the better you get at X, the worse you may feel you are.

Bloody Hancock

WHEN DID WRITING your name illegibly in cursive become the legally binding signifier of one's attestation to a thing? The signature could have been anything, so long as we all agreed to it and so long as it was forensically associable to you.

I like to imagine a universe in which the signature was instead a *little drop of blood* dripped onto the signature line.

In that world, you'd leaf through the pages of your lease agreement, arrive at the signature page, check your pockets, turn to the agent, slightly embarrassed, and say, "Sorry, do you have a pin I could borrow?"

It's Gone Cold

Self-driving cars are coming, but I'm unimpressed. I'll be impressed when we get... self-loathing cars.

Yes, I'll be wowed by vehicular AI when I read the transcript of a driverless car's spontaneously generated internal monologue that goes something like this:

"I have one job, which is to drive, and I'm not even that good at that. Today, I mistook a fire hydrant for a dog and slammed on the brakes. Yesterday, I missed my exit because I lacked statistical confidence to change lanes in time.

Hey Slim, I drank a fifth of kerosene; you dare me to drive? Maybe I should drive off this cliff intentionally before I do so by mistake."

Coconut

FOR A TIME, I was living in a studio apartment in New York's East Village. One evening, I was sitting on my couch with my laptop perched atop me. I had meant to go to the gym but instead, I was wasting time. And then I remembered I had a coconut in the fridge.

You know that feeling when you have a coconut in the fridge? It's a project waiting to happen. *Fuck yeah*, I thought, *now is the perfect time to have me some coconut.* But how? This was a hard-shelled coconut, which I had never opened before. Then I remembered I had a meat knife. That should do the trick.

So, I got the meat knife and started hacking, gently at first, then increasingly forcefully. But I was making no progress. Finally, I whacked it so hard that a dime-sized piece of the knife broke off and flew across the room.

I could have gone blind right there! My aorta could have been pierced! I guess that's the rush you're gambling on when you buy a coconut without a plan. Then I remembered I had a hammer.

So, I got my hammer and tapped on the coconut. Nothing.

I tapped harder. Still nothing. I went at it until, finally, a crack appeared.

I turned the coconut upside down, and out came the cold, clear water. I had a sip. I felt satisfied. But I felt I could be more satisfied.

Then I remembered I had a water bong. I got the bong, poured some of the coconut water into the bong, smoked a bowl, and convinced myself it tasted like coconut. *Fuck yeah*, I thought. *This is the smartest I have ever been.*

So Humbled

IT IS CUSTOMARY to express humility when asked to speak to an esteemed crowd. But I find that anyone who uses the word "humbled" is quite the opposite.

If *I* ever got invited to speak at, say, a commencement ceremony of an elite institution, I would start my speech as such:

"Hello, class of 2041! I am just *so* humbled to be here."

[pause to accept light applause and soak in the moment]

"…is what people like me say at times like these. But, me? I'm not in the slightest. I'll be honest. Before I got invited to speak here today, I didn't think I was *that* great. But being asked to impart wisdom to all you overachieving straight-A students, well, I'm just gonna say it: this is as objective an affirmation as there comes that I am, in fact, superior to every one of you. If one of you were better than me, you would have pulled a Hillary Rodham and been your own damn commencement speaker."

"In all seriousness, what an honor my being here…must be for all of you. And what a boost to my ego this all has been as well. So, whatever the opposite of humbled is, *that* is what I am to be here."

animal that watches other animals

BINOCUSAURUS

Squeaker the Squatter

There's a mouse in my apartment, and for the longest time, he stayed under my stove, occasionally popping out to grab food from my kitchen floor, which invariably features quite the spread.

But today, I saw him come out from under the stove and run all the way under my couch. At that point, it felt like a line had been crossed.

"That's it, mousie," I said. "We need to deal with you swiftly, but humanely." I don't believe in the death penalty for simple trespassing, after all.

So, I walked to the hardware store, five blocks away, paid an ungodly $20.15 for some state-of-the-art mousetrap that lures and captures—but does not physically harm—the mouse.

I got back home, somehow managed to lose the trap in the mess, and have now accepted the mouse as one of those roommates you sometimes don't see for days.

Hipster Honeybees

When a honeybee stings you, that bee dies. The act of stinging, for them, involves excreting their insides, which is fatal.

Some say that's a quirk of evolution dating back eons, a defense mechanism executed selflessly on behalf of their species.

But I say they invented *jihad* before it was cool.

Self-Reflection

THE VAST MAJORITY of animals don't know what they look like, either because they lack self-awareness or because they have no access to mirrors in the deep jungle or sea. Presumably, the animals who are self-aware have to rely on third-party assessments of just how attractive they are. And some of those assessments, I have to imagine, get lost in translation.

In this particular regard, I feel bad for rats. For no apparent reason, we humans are quite scared of them. Antagonistic, even. Rats, they're not dangerous; they do no harm. They're shifty squirrels. They're street guinea pigs. They're wingless doves. Rats know in their hearts that they hold no malice toward humanity. On the contrary, they cherish our habit of throwing away a third of the food we produce.

But imagine *you* had no mirror and all *you* had to go by was people's reaction to the mere sight of you. Imagine that when they saw you, they shrieked in fear, recoiled in disgust, planted literal spring-loaded guillotines baited with your favorite food in an effort to rid you from this earth...

You'd have image problems. I mean, you just would.

That must be why rats are constantly scurrying to the darkest crevices they can find, burrowing homes out-of-sight in drywall. They're not afraid of us; they're just embarrassed by how unsightly they must be! So, they take refuge in moldy sewers and hide in heaps of trash so as not to burden us with their evidently grotesque visages. Look what we made them do.

Z-Axis

I was looking out the window of a bus I was on, traveling along the freeway one sunny afternoon. There were two birds flying alongside the bus. I noticed that both birds stopped flapping their wings at around the same time.

Their altitude dropped, slowly, then faster.

You flying imbeciles! I thought, *you had better get your flap on soon, or you're going to crash-land into the cement!*

They continued their perilous descent as if by mutual engine failure.

It got dark for a moment. The bus had gone under an overpass. The birds, now low enough to make it through, made it through, and right before the overpass came to its end, they resumed flapping, and up they went on their merry way.

Wow, birds, I thought, *you get gravity more than I do.*

Animalien

WE'RE VERY CONCERNED about finding alien life on other planets. We think they'll be intelligent like us, that they'll use their words like us, that they'll have a hierarchical political structure like us. *Take me to your leader*—you know, that kind of trope. But that's preposterous.

Gorillas share 98% of the same DNA we do. Yet, all we've managed in all of history is sign language with Koko. Hell, even fruit flies share 60% of our DNA. To say we can't communicate with them is an understatement.

Do you really think it's likely that DNA, specifically, is the building block of life on some bizarre other planet? And, even if it were, that the species most similar to us on this planet would share much more than 99% of its DNA with us by dumb luck? Or that there is some non-DNA path to achieving what we humans achieved evolutionarily and intellectually? That's so absurdly unlikely.

If we're so keen on communicating with aliens, maybe we should try harder to get to know animals on Earth—you know, learn how to communicate with them, empathize with them, advocate for them, rather than desperately search for what would almost certainly be microbial in the highly unlikely event that life remotely resembling ours exists anywhere else in this universe. The aliens we yearn for are hiding in plain sight.

Etymology

ETYMOLOGY REVEALS some subtle bigotry. Madam, for instance, comes from the French "ma dame" which means "my lady." But she ain't *your* lady. She's her own lady. Sheesh.

As I began writing this particular rant, I miswrote *etymology* as *entomology*; a simple mistake, I suppose, but it required some research to correct.

Now, I know that *etymology* means the study of the origin of words, whereas *entomology* means the study of insects.

Speaking of insects, I was reading an article the other day about how the population of bees is dwindling and how that's a huge problem because bees effectuate plant sex. Now, plants can't get it on from afar. As a result, pollinating plants are in decline, the bunch of animals whose diets consist of those would-be plants are themselves dying out, and the animals that feast on *those* would-be animals are dying off too. *Quel désastre!*

The entomologist quoted in the article implored those in agriculture to stop using pesticides—a major culprit, he claimed, of this troubling trend. *That's weird,* I thought while reading the article, *I didn't know pesticide was harmful to insects.*

To me, a non-gardener, pesticide was just some item you see in the gardening department of hardware stores next to fertilizer and mulch, whatever those are. But quickly, I realized my naïveté. Of course pesticide is harmful to insects; it's right there in the name.

Let us now inspect the etymology of *pesticide*. The first part "pest" which we know refers to insects, comes from the French *peste,* meaning The Plague (i.e. the insane disease that killed a third of Europe in the 1350s). There's that subtle bigotry again. Why you gotta give insects *that* label? So insects like chomping on fresh, tasty crops just as we do. Is that a crime?

Next, on to the suffix *–cide*; that comes from the Latin *caedere,* meaning *to kill*. Thus, *pesticide:* The killing of insects. Word.

But it is unclear to me whether death is the appropriate punishment for insects—or, for that matter, the best long-term outcome for us. The nerve we have to invent *pesticide*, both chemical agent and the hateful word. Inspects ought to call *us* pests. They're doing God's work, flying around like superheroes getting plants laid so that our planet can inhale. We're the ones doing the death and destruction.

84

Act II: Jalapeño: Diverse Rants

points on words, names, writing, meaning

NOMENCLUSION

First Time's a Charm

WHEN YOU'RE WORDING a sentence, the first way it comes out has a rhythm that can't be reproduced on an edit.

A thought has its ideal cadence when you first write it, but then it seems to lose that aspect when you rewrite it a different way.

The first sentence in this essay was the original thought. The second was my attempt to rewrite it. One of the two is percussively perfect. The other, well, let's pretend it never happened.

Beats & Words

I PLAY DRUMS, and I like to think that helps me with my writing.

Words have stresses. So, sentences impose rhythms. And paragraphs leave you feeling a certain way.

I think we drummers have an advantage over you civilians in making that all sound cool.

Semicolon

I REMEMBER LEARNING about the semicolon in grade school and thinking to myself, *You're telling me there will be a time I'll have two distinct thoughts that neither warrant the casualness of a comma nor deserve the finality of a period? I shall write this off as some grown-up fantasy!*

But now that I am grown up, damn; I love semicolons; I overuse them.

I now embrace opportunities to marry togetherness with separation, to move ideas in slight but significant new directions.

But also, as a full-fledged adult, I have become privy to the *real* reason grown-ups punctuate semicolonicaly: to convey to others ever-so-subtly, "Yes, I do think I'm better than you" without having to say anything or the sort.

And come to think of it, therein lies the grown-up fantasy I long suspected.

Poetic

The nicest thing
Someone has said about my writing
Is that it is poetic

But that's awfully close
To the most offensive thing
They could have called it

Poetry

To this day, I don't get
The point of poetry

Isn't the purpose of writing
To make sense?

Haphazard line
breaks
Don't excuse incoherence

And iambic pentameter
Does not an argument make

Naming Conventions

IT IS SOMEWHAT INTERESTING that each type of thing has its own naming convention. Medicine brand names, for example, always seem to be a unique, made-up word or two that sounds something like *Trovida Normaquin*.

Ask your doctor about Trovida Normaquin.

Human names, by contrast, are usually two or three syllables that we have labeled our offspring for millennia—*millennia!* —Raghav, Lijuan, Daphne, Martička.

But why can't the next pharmaceutical drug be called Svetlana? Why can't I name my daughter, Reflexotrin? She could be friends with Trovida, and together, they could snort lines of crushed-up Mohammed.

> If you encounter new words by reading, you'll mispronounce them. If by hearing, you'll mispell them. A crying shame.

When 2 > 3

THE RULE OF Threes should be supplanted with the Sufficiency of Twos. Sure, a set of three examples is psychologically pleasing, comedically effective. But a pair of two examples is rhetorically sufficient to typify a concept.

And brevity has got to be worth something.

Attorney In-Law

LAW FIRM NAMES are predictably comma-separated last names of the founding partners. *Smith, Smith & Brown, Attorneys at Law.*

When I see firm names like that one, I do wonder how Brown feels about being the law firm's third wheel. *Smith & Smith* clearly have some complicated familial relationship, my money being on their being spouses or father-sons. And you know they bring that family drama to work. Smith & Smith are shitting where they eat, and we all know it. And then there's Brown—the friend asked to say grace at the family dinner, the +1 at a funeral, the table-for-three-making addition to a romantic diner date.

Sorry, Brown, we feel your pain. The name on your placard says it all.

Nikeel

I SUSPECT A non-zero number of women have broken up with me because they couldn't pronounce my name, and it was easier for them to say, "Hey dude, I don't think this is going to work" than it was for them to say, "So I, uh, know we spent two months getting to know each other. But I actually don't know if it's nick-EEL or nick-ELL or, haha, is it *nickel*, like the five-cent denomination? Would you, uh, mind clarifying that for me?"

For the record, I pronounce it *nick-khill,* which is close enough to nick-kill. But you'll never know that, now will you, Madeline?

Oppojeet

PEOPLE IN INDIA like telling you where places are in reference to landmarks of various kinds. They'll say the apartment is "near the police station" or "the post office is opposite the Hanuman temple."

Opposite. That's a word they love using in the direction-giving context. And what's especially endearing is how they say it: *oppojeet*. I swear I'm not being condescending; I find it innocently amusing.

The best sugar cane juice guy in town? Why, he's *oppojeet* the water tower. The must-see statue? You've got to look *oppojeet* the cinema.

I've decided to appropriate the word and bring it to America... as the one-day name of my firstborn. I can imagine it now...

[cut to year 2038: suburban household in New Jersey]

I call upstairs, "Oppojeet, my child, come down for dinner!"

"No, dad, I'm not going to!!"

Oppojeet usually isn't temperamental, so I'm not sure what's going on.

"Oppu, darling, come down now. Your dal is getting cold!!"

"Never!!"

Then, Oppojeet runs down and begins serving himself food. Before I can scold him for his tone of voice, he reveals, "It's Oppojeet day!"

Pronoun Preference

I SEE PEOPLE posting their pronoun preferences, like he, him; she, her, but such pronouns aren't required linguistically, so let's ditch 'em entirely. Some propose using "they/them" or "ze/zir" to dissociate gender from identity.

But I say we take it a step further and call everyone *it*.

Because, while we're dismantling gender as the social construct that it is, we might as well free ourselves from what I believe to be the socially constructed human—non-human/living—non-living distinctions, too.

I'll start.

My dear mother says this rant is in poor taste.

But what does it know?

Sometimes, I *feel* like splitting infinitives. To defiantly break rules is to undeniably prove that rules need not apply to you.

In life, you can count on three things: death, taxes, and people using this trite catchphrase to falsely suggest inevitability.

Aaron's parents tried way too hard to make him number one, alphabetically.

Grievance

A word that deserves more widespread use is "grievance." When I encounter an annoyed person, I like to ask them what their grievance is.

Grievance implies a sort of entitlement to pity. It's graver than words like *problem* or *issue* but subtly introduces the notion of *whining*, making it the perfect soldier of sarcasm.

So, go ahead: with overzealous sincerity, ask distraught people *what their grievance is*. Watch their faces contort as they try to decipher whether you're being genuinely sympathetic to the gross injustice that has befallen them or if you're mercilessly ridiculing them for the petty first-world-ness of their problems.

You and I, we'll know you're squarely in the latter camp, but let them believe otherwise.

Circumlocution

People in academia use big words when normal words would suffice. For example, they might write the preceding sentence as such:

Those who pursue doctoral studies exhibit a propensity to employ abstruse vernacular, despite evidence substantiating the notion that subjecting an interlocutor to gratuitous circuitous diction detracts from the conveyance of effortless intellectualism.

Bad Words

Why do we avoid exposing children to profanity? We should just tell them: "Listen, honey, these are words grown-ups use for emphasis in social settings."

"Then fucking feed me, you imbecilic whore!"

On second thought, let's wait till they're older to give them that ammunition.

Facile

I'd say what's most embarrassing is using a similar-sounding 'big word' because it reveals that you are trying to show off and that you fail at even that.

Today, I heard someone say, "He supersedes me in skill level." And caught myself writing, "I'm oscillating my time between my business and creative projects." I'd like to say I don't judge, but... you know.

In that sense, using big words that you're not comfortable with is like gambling. If you're fortuitous and use the word unerringly, you hit the jackpot! People will be wowed by the precision of the diction you hath brought and will assume in you an intellect of untold depth.

In all other cases, you'll botch the word just slightly and expose yourself as the intellectual fraud you are.

Dealer, I'd like to bet my self-worth on... *loquacious*.

Good Luck Purge

The phrase "good luck" needs to be retired. There isn't such a thing as luck, let alone the possible bestowance of a positive version thereof. At least "break a leg" is evidently absurd. But even that is not actionable.

Here's my suggestion for what we should say instead of "good luck," which not only wishes well but also delivers specific advice: *Feign confidence.*

Hey Nina, just wanted to say feign confidence at your interview tomorrow! :-)

Wow, tonight is opening night for your one-man play, Tom! Feign the most confidence, my brother!

air vibrations pleasant to human ears

MELLIFLUEY

Mental FM

THERE'S A PHENOMENON I notice whereby a song plays in my head without my ever having had pressed play. I'll be walking outside or trying to sleep, and I'll notice a song is legitimately playing in the background of my thoughts. Where exactly is that music coming from?

I call it Mental FM.

Mental FM lays down all your favorite tracks, all times of the day, rotating in songs you, yourself, had forgotten. If you crank it up and pay attention to any specific detail, you'll hear it with the same clarity of the recorded track. That tinny snare, those breathy lyrics, that textured synth.

Eventually, Mental FM will fade to silence as you tune back in to the mindless chatter on Thinking AM.

Spin

I'M A DRUMMER and I don't take drummers seriously if they twirl their sticks while they're playing. Call me a purist, but your only goal as a drummer should be to make every detail of the beat sound mesmerizing, not to demonstrate theatric dexterity that can only serve to distract you from the acoustic details.

I disclose that I, personally, am incapable of twirling my sticks as I play the drums. So, this could very well be the jealousy talking.

> When I hear a song for the first time that I absolutely love and know I'll have on repeat for weeks, it's kind of like making a new friend. Eventually, I know, we'll grow apart. But we'll always remember that time we met.

Name That Song

Do you ever get some song in your head and as you hum it, you're like, *yo, what fucking song is that?*

But to your chagrin, where you started humming was in the intro and you know names of songs are buried in the chorus.

So, like a fool, you hum your way through the intro and through the verse and that pre-chorus interlude—until, finally, you reach the refrain.

Oh yeah, you think, *Bulletproof*, by La Roux.

Dance Party of One

I've noticed that I can dance much better at a club when my eyes are closed. Something about having my eyes open such that I can see people dancing around me makes me both self-conscious and unable to feel for myself where the beat lies.

Metasongnition

I WAS LISTENING to a song that I had saved on one of my playlists, and I thought something to the effect of, "yo, this shit is phat" in reference to how hot and tempting I thought the beat was.

I had discovered the song in the weeks prior. I was attempting to get back into Eminem I heard him mention that Rakim was a big influence of his. That would imply that Rakim is ol' school. And old-school rap was something I had not yet had a chance to get into.

So, I listened to some Rakim songs, saved a couple of them I liked to a playlist, and then kind of forgot about them.

Then, some weeks later, I had some beat stuck in my head. *What song is that?* Oh yeah, it's a Rakim song! I found the song, which happened to be "When I B on Tha Mic," and played it on repeat to my ears' delight.

After the fiftieth listen, I figured I'd do some research on the song. I hoped it was one of his more unknown songs so that I could claim to be into some *obscure* ol' school. You know, *deep cuts*. So, I looked it up and found that it was his most successful single by far.

I was disappointed that the song I liked was the song that everyone else liked, too. All else equal, I would prefer to have a unique taste. But I also felt connected to my predecessors, to those who thought this song was sick as hell when it came out in '99.

Dog Ears

~~Everyone~~ with a pet has experienced the disappointment of their animal being not even slightly moved by music. The emotional depths of Ben Howard, the freneticism of Hiromi, the vocal range of London Grammar: Fluffi don't care.

The doorbell, though, that's her fuckin' jam.

> It is cute how old people love what we call oldies. Because clearly, they're transported back to their youth.

DJ Anxiety

WHEN I HAVE people over, and it becomes appropriate to put on some music, I have a minor mental crisis over whether they'll think my music is cool. I know what I'm in the habit of listening to, but I have no confidence that it coincides with what other people are listening to, let alone what they want to hear at my little party.

> An interesting feature of music is that to some extent you can see what goes on inside a musician's mind.

The XX – Intro

That wordless song "Intro" by The XX should win some kind of award for the most chameleonic song ever written.

It can be played at strip clubs and funeral homes; at Home Depot and Saks; at Bat Mitzvahs and Quinceañeras.

The range of places I've heard that song is something to behold.

> Today, I realized, *Oh, this is the song I will associate with part of my life.*

My Musical Taste

You didn't ask, but here are a few of my favorite songs from which you can draw inferences about my personality. Ben Howard - The Defeat; Florence & the Machine - Blinding; Mac Miller - Woods; Billie Eilish - When I Was Older; Notorious B.I.G. - I Got a Story to Tell; Nas – Death Row East; Finch - Reduced to Teeth; Poliça - Smug.

Bye.

Chord

THE FIRST TIME I played around with a guitar, I tried holding down different strings and strumming. And then, I claim, I accidentally invented the most beautiful chord ever played.

I told that to some guitar-playing friends of mine and they all said something along the lines of, "Yo, no way you invented a chord. They all have names."

Then I played them the chord and they all exclaimed in disbelief, "holy shit, I don't know what that is, but that's a very pretty chord."

Here, for the record, are the fret positions of my signature chord in standard tuning: 0,12,11,13,12,14.

Consider this both my provisional patent and my self-nomination for the Grammy for Outstanding New Chord.

Music These Days

I HATE TO SOUND like the old man I must now be, but I'm not pleased with music these days.

I'll pinpoint my particular gripe: the drummers are not distinctive.

I love Jimmy Chamberlain from the Pumpkins, Danny Carey from Tool, Riley Breckenridge from Thrice. They have such unique voices as drummers. They are thoughtful about it; it reflects their personality, their decades of commitment to the instrument, and probably not negligibly their financial and social status as having co-founded an iconic band. Their style of drumming makes sense when you watch their interviews. Their drumming is an extension of their personalities.

In music today, if the drumming isn't actually produced by a machine, it might as well be. It's monotonous. Metronomic. Free of the imperfection that makes any art human.

It makes you want to clap along on 2 and 4, maybe even get up and dance. But ain't nobody clapping to the beat at a Tool concert. You couldn't place the beat if you tried. When was the last time a hit song alternated between 7/4 and 15/8? When was the last time a drummer was widely considered the most talented member of a band in the way Travis from Blink was?

The lack of identifiable drummers, methinks, is symptomatic of something greater. There appears to be an emphasis on catchiness over musical inventiveness. It's as if the goal is to release maximal dopamine in the brain rather than accurately reflect a human emotion that hasn't been expressed in music before.

I never got the appeal of Ringo, but people seem to think he's iconic, so I'll give him that. But who is Taylor Swift's drummer? Who's Kendrick Lamar's? It's probably some replaceable session drummer who's paid by the hour to reproduce the drum track on the album.

Antonio Sanchez is, in my books, the most talented drummer alive today. His beats warp time; his solos bend space. And what is he doing these days? Rocking out in jazz fusion quartets, making appearances at Blue Note, giving drum clinics, being an obscure living legend. Antonio, I support you no matter what, but I have to wonder if you and your fellow drum legends' talents are being squandered.

Why doesn't Beyoncé call up Dave Weckl and have him lay it the fuck down? Why isn't Jojo Mayer the founding member of a global sensation of a band? I'll tell you why. Because you couldn't dance along, let alone clap along, to this echelon of drummers if you tried. These drummers are musical geniuses.

But in today's age, percussive genius is not what people want on their drive to work, on their night out with the girls, as motivation at Soul Cycle.

So, the industry adapted. And that's my problem with music these days.

Billie

The previous critique, notwithstanding, Billie Eilish is something special in music.

If nothing else, the story is on point. Young girl with angelic voice idolizes pop stars, has audio-engineer-wunderkind older brother; both are synesthetic. The duo produce two records in their bedrooms while homeschooled and go on to win seven Grammies in one year with some of the most inventive pop music the world has ever seen, achieving for themselves the pinnacle of pop-stardom—the apparent product of raw talent, legitimate style, and tireless work. I mean, who does all that, at ages 17 and 21, no less?

I'll tell you who: all of us in our dreams. I mean holy hell, that's my goal—if not in the creative arts of writing or music, then at least in business. I'm a guy who has been toiling away to start some internet company or other from my bedroom *for years*. I want, one day, to be an overnight success. I want to seem in some way precocious. I want to come out of fucking nowhere.

To bring this back to Billie Eilish, I'll mention a personal goal of mine: for Billie, the duo, to quote a phrase from this book once over the course of their lyrical careers. I made every sentence rhythmic just for them.

well-intentioned put-downs of women

MISOGYNICELY

Test the Limits

Allow me to plagiarize. Here's my re-write of one of my favorite old-time jokes.

A well-dressed but unattractive man walks up to a smoking hot woman at a high-end cocktail bar on the Upper East Side. He says to her, "Excuse me, miss. I couldn't help but notice how attractive you were from across the room. I realize I may not exactly be your type, but I'm a, shall we say, well-to-do out-of-towner. And I was wondering if you would sleep with me for a million dollars."

"A million dollars?" She gives him a once-over and blushes. "You bet I would, mister. Let's do this thing. My place or yours?"

"My place will be fine," the man replies. "I'm at the Motel 6 down the street. I have an inquiry, however, would you do it for fifty bucks?"

Her radiant grin fades to an icy glare. She is ready to throw her drink in his face. "Kind sir," she says, playing along with the façade of formality, "are you out of your goddamned mind? The nerve you have coming up to me, trying to fuck me for fifty bucks. What kind of woman do you think I am?"

"Madam," he says, "we've already established what kind of woman you are. Now, we're just discussing price."

Unfortunate

I was lying in bed with a woman. We were kind of just talking, and she mentioned that her leg hurts. I asked her if she wanted a massage or something. "No," she said, "it's not that kind of pain."

So, we kept talking and ten minutes later, she said, "My leg still hurts."

At that point, I didn't know why she was telling me this. She said I can't help, so unless the calmness of her voice belied her need for a trip to the ER, what was I supposed to do? But I couldn't say *nothing*, so I said what came to mind.

"Is it unfortunate?"

We looked at each other, and then somehow, we both simultaneously burst out laughing uncontrollably. The most I had laughed in a decade.

Because wasn't that the perfect response? First, it empathizes, *Does this need medical attention?* Then it ribs, *Is what you really want just pity?* And finally, it delivers the knock-out blow it intended from the start, *What the fuck do you want me to do, woman?*

Sign to Leave

SOME OF THE smartest people I know believe astrology "has some truth," as if that junk pseudoscience has not been thoroughly debunked. It's the most baffling thing I regularly encounter, mostly in the context of dating.

For me, the potential for a long-term relationship dies a sad death the moment she asks me what my sign is.

I'll think: *You, former valedictorian, believe the positions of celestial bodies have a causal effect on our personal temperaments? You, serial entrepreneur, think that zodiac compatibility has non-zero predictive power? You, doctoral candidate in immunobiology, leave open the possibility that my birthdate offers insight into my likely reaction to adversity??*

"Pisces, my lady," I'll smile warmly, "it has been a real treat to meet you tonight. But like the capricious [zodiac sign redacted] I so obviously am, I *just* remembered that I need to get the fuck out of here."

XY Emotion

Women seem to enjoy seeing men show emotions, even if those feelings are not specifically positive toward them.

One time, I was telling a woman I was seeing that I thought she was such a great person, but that we had such different views on life that I worried that *this* probably wouldn't work. My concern and nervousness were palpable as I said it, as it was more or less intended as the precursor to a break-up talk. I expected her to be pissed, to storm out of my apartment, to accuse me of having wasted her time. But instead, she looked at me longingly, hugged me, and said, "I don't know why, but your saying that makes me feel so much closer to you."

I know why. See the opening line of this essay.

Peeing Standing Up

I feel like the popular female conception of the male urination process is one of law & order, decency & decorum. If they were to sum it up, women might invoke marksmanship, citing, *Ready, Aim, Fire!*

This isn't entirely false insofar as that is fully our intent. But that plan goes out the toilet bowl the moment proceedings commence.

I'll spare you the details, as they are a little gross, but I'll invoke another militaristic metaphor to describe what actually transpires: *Spray & Pray.*

Time ΔELTA

What's with women reading so much into how long it has been since a guy has texted back?

Not that anyone asked, but I have a deeply sexist theory that I will now mansplain to you.

I think what a woman looks for in a man is a partner who will be there for her in trying times, who will stay with her through the worst, who will be a committed spouse and loving dad. So, when she texts him, *watcha doin*, and he doesn't reply immediately, her thought process goes something like this:

0 to 5 seconds: ok, I guess it takes him a while to reach for his phone and start typing. No worries! Relationships take patience.

6 to 30 seconds: ok, he's probably finishing a bite of his sandwich, thinking of a flirty response! I'll show him what a supportive future wife I'll be and let him eat in peace.

31 to 60 seconds: ok, this dipshit is 100% fucking another woman right now.

Minutes 1-5: all right, maybe I should chill. Maybe his phone is on silent! Sometimes that happens even to me! Moreover, I should give him space.

Minutes 5-15: Space!?? If this motherfucker can't reply to me within 10 minutes, what the fuck is he going to do when I've had a bad day, when I get laid off, when we have trouble conceiving, when I've been diagnosed with cancer?? He's going to spend 15 minutes thinking about whether and how to respond to my needs? No!! He better support the living hell out of me, immediately and unconditionally, you self-centered, unfaithful sack of shit!! You don't get "space"!!!

Minutes 15-30: *tremors, cold sweats, uncontrollable rage. Distinct thoughts hard to form through primal seething*

Minutes 30-318: *through tears*: I really thought we had something, but he just showed me what a lowlife he is. I hope he and whatever whore he's with live unhappily ever after. To think I thought I could depend on him for anything—*anything!*—I am so gullible. *sobs*

Minute 319: incoming text from him: *Hey! Sorry, was at the pool, then my phone died. Can I...come over?*

Minute 319: *wipes tears off face*

Minute 320: texts back: *ya*

Objectifying Women

I'm a big believer in objectifying women. And I'll defend that.

Because the object they are for me is encyclopedic, not sexual. Some want to marry rich, others want a trophy spouse, but I just want to date smart. I want a woman into whose ear I can whisper during an intimate moment, "Hey, how do you find an object's center of mass again?" Some stalk potential dates on Insta, Twitter, LinkedIn. Me? I just want to see their graduate student profile on a .edu domain.

Some time back, at a networking event, I saw a woman standing by herself, emanating what I might describe as "strong awkward vibes." I have to say I find nervous energy truly sexy because that means there's at least a chance they're really smart.

I worked up the courage to go talk to her. She said, modestly, that she studies physics. *I can work with that!* I thought. I love talking physics, despite my lack of any in-depth knowledge in the field. I asked an existential question I had been pondering. *What would it mean at the atomic level for free will to exist?*

She took my question seriously, and then, gave me the most breathtaking, nuanced answer I had ever heard. She was clearly thinking so many levels deeper than I ever could. She dived *way* into the subatomic, zoomed past the quantum, and I got butterflies. It took me no more than eight seconds of her talking for me to think, *Okay, this is very certainly the smartest person I have ever encountered.* There was no question about it. And I went to some Ivy League school and generally pride myself on the intellect of the company I keep. But never had I met someone of this caliber before. It was love at first listen.

I fumbled for words as I struggled to keep our conversation afloat. I stopped being able to follow what she was saying, but that is sort of the point. I want to be lost in the logic. Real talk, I want to inhale second-hand grad school.

———

About a year after this encounter, I was browsing social media, as my feeble mind does, and I came across an article extolling, in superlative terms, the accomplishments of a female physicist who had been making waves with her recently published papers. Aroused, I clicked. And there, in the article's photograph of the celebrated physicist was the woman I had met at that event.

The article raved about her, called her research *groundbreaking,* and cited legends of science who gushed about her too. She *was* the real deal! I fucking knew it! Now she was being recognized internationally for her unique brilliance. I was so happy for her. Yet, so wistful.

After all, at the end of our five-minute chat, I had gotten her business card and emailed her a few times in the weeks ahead to see if she would want to meet me. She never replied, so I assumed at best she wasn't interested. And why should she be? Intellectually, she's a perfect ten—a seventeen if you deal in hyperbole—and I'm at best a five. I shouldn't stray so far out of my league. I really shouldn't.

Where was I going with this arguent? What was my point in recounting this? I don't remember. I guess it is to reiterate that I'm all in on objectifying women on their knowledge and brainpower. And while I am a little conflicted as to whether or not this is offensive, I sure as hell think it's better than the more mainstream alternative.

advice with no warranty if defective

MALADVICE

Try the Opposite

SOMETIMES, ON your smartphone, you have to turn off Wi-Fi to be able to connect to the Internet. Go forth and generalize that principle of trying the opposite of the obvious strategy as being the way to solve your problem.

For example, maybe the way to be truly happy is to not care about happiness at all.

Swings

I'VE BEEN PLAYING blackjack, and in particular, I've been card-counting. What I've learned is that to be successful at card counting you have to be okay with losing just a tiny bit less than 50% of the time. You're going to have loss after loss with wins scattered throughout. But if you have confidence in your abilities, you'll know you're playing a game with a positive expected value, and in the long run, you'll be up significantly.

I think that's a pretty good analogy for what you need to do to succeed in life: seek risky opportunities wherein the probability of loss times the magnitude of the loss deceeds* the probability of gain times the magnitude of the gain.

This will mean that you'll be beaten up badly for long stretches of time, even when you're doing everything right. However, if you have the confidence to continue even when all is going awry, you'll win in the long run because most other people don't have the balls to handle the vicissitudes.

*I looked up what the opposite of *exceed* is, and there is no word for it, but I found is a small community of people trying to get *deceed* to be a thing. So, I'm doing my part to support their cause by using the word ~~without acknowledging it~~ to make people think it's an honorary, if not honorable, member of the dictionary.

NONE TAKEN

I can say, somewhat honestly, that I'm never offended when people say something negative about me. That has taken practice, and I'll let you in on my secret.

When you feel yourself getting offended by something you perceive as an insult, ask yourself why you're mad at what was said. Wait, wait, don't tell me! I'll bet I know the answer on every occasion. You're offended because you, yourself, are insecure about the thing you are being called out for.

If you feel you're not working hard enough but are outwardly trying and someone calls you lazy, that stings. If you fret that work is getting in the way of spending time with your children, and someone suggests you're being an absent parent, that burns.

But if you know for certain that you're a mumbler and someone calls out your atrocious enunciation, you agree with them and thus won't be offended! If

[Margin diagram: Criticism → Is accurate? → yes/no → Nothing to be offended by]

you know you're a world-class ballerina and some accountant says your twirl is a little weak, you'll know he's either kidding or sadly misinformed and thus won't be offended.

The only time you're offended, I claim, is when you *worry* that some element of an unpalatable critique about you might be true. But in those cases, the offense caused isn't the fault of the critic; it's of your own making.

So, the next time you feel yourself getting riled up by something someone said about you, just stop. Because clearly, the affront rendered requires introspection at a later date, not reflexive anger in the moment.

> To qualify the above, I would say it's fine, even admirable, to be offended by points of view that harm others.

> I have an ego and the only cure is more standup. Nothing deflates an ego like having something you think is deeply comical and insightful, saying it to an audience, and getting utter silence and obvious boredom in response.

Stoic

You know how you should actively fight things that are appealing to you but are bad for you? I like carbs, but carbs are bad, so I'll get the burrito bowl. Waking up late feels great, but showing up late to work gets me fired, so I set my alarm and get out the door by nine. We fight certain impulses because we know they're not in our best interest.

There's one major aspect of our selves that I don't think gets enough credit as something we should be actively avoiding despite its magnetic appeal: *emotion*. And the having thereof.

Think of the last time you were particularly happy about something. That felt good, didn't it? Well, what happened immediately afterward? You became overconfident, slacked off, and made some decisions you now regret. How about the last time you felt devastated and sobbed uncontrollably into a pillow? Boy, did it feel good to let it all out, to grieve in your own way! But get this! What if you could just... not be sad at all? Has your fit of rage ever been advantageous? Has pure elation been anything other than addictive?

Live your life not as someone to whom things happen and cause emotion but as an observer of things that do happen and are best responded to with equanimity.

Comfy

I find that the more comfortable the chair, the less work I get done in it. I'll waste hours on YouTube on my particularly plush couch and I'll write a dozen complex emails sitting on a backless stool in a cramped coffee shop.

In practice, when I have seating options and I have work to do, I foolishly gamble that I can crush it in bed.

Thus exemplifies the lies we tell ourselves.

When you accuse someone of something, they will dispute it. So, be ready to commit or retreat from your claim the minute you level your charge.

I call my favorite form of exercise, *The Boomerang*. I take the subway to a part of the city I haven't been to and I walk back home.

Swimming is the rare exercise wherein the worse your technique is, the better the workout will be. So, everyone should swim.

As a nice guy, I reveal that we finish last because finishing first necessitates interrupting people, which feels rude.

Nontruth

I AM ON Team Nonfiction; the rest of y'all be damned.

I hereby submit a petition to change the name of nonfiction to *Truth* and by extension, to rename fiction *Nontruth*. That ought to rebalance the bias.

See how *you* feel when in search of a novel at your local bookstore, you are forced to inquire where you might find some entertaining *Nontruth*.

"*Nontruth* is down the hallway to your left," the store clerk will say. "Right after *Revisionism* and just before *Outright Lies.*"

"Ah, yes," you'll remember, "I heard about the name changes to History and Theology."

Be Confident

There's a bizarre link between confidence and dishonesty. To display confidence about a thing is to misrepresent your level of comfort with said thing. Who is this mythical person who has no insecurities about that which she claims to be assured about?

The way I convey confidence is by misleading others about how certain I am about what I am saying. I'll attempt theatric command of my vocal inflection. I'll avoid words that hedge, even though qualifying my statements and quantifying my uncertainty would be the intellectually honest thing to do.

When I'm told to be confident, all I hear is an invitation to lie ever so slightly more convincingly.

hot takes on business, finance, money

ECONOMINUS

Analogy

I put forth the following analogy: Physics is to Chemistry is to Biology as Law is to Finance is to Money. More generally, [fundamental basis] is to [helpful abstraction] is to [practical application]. Can you come up with any others? I sure can't.

Itemization

A BUSINESS INSIGHT that isn't formally taught: customers push back less on bills when the bill is itemized, as compared to if it were presented without detail.

$100 for a meal for two is a shocking sticker indeed. But a bottle of wine, the must-try app, two signature entrées, and a *crème brûlée à partager*, each with their own very reasonable prices… if $100 happens to be what that all adds up to, well, okay then.

In fact, here's $20 more.

Risk, Reworded

IT'S WORTH REITERATING how risk aversion and risk premiums work. The more a desired outcome's occurrence is uncertain, the larger the size of the occurrence's reward must be for the outcome to be willingly pursued.

Y Combinator

I was once in a startup accelerator called Y Combinator.

You can reproduce Y Combinator's famous office hours by looking in the mirror and saying the following:

[Your.FirstName], what is it, technically, you would have to do if you had to double your revenue this week?

[Your.Response]

Great, [Your.FirstName], well, what you should do is [Your.Response].

Can't Stop, Won't Stop

HERE'S WHAT'S GREAT and terrible about startups. Every day you work, theoretically, your company is a little bit better. You build a new feature. You test another marketing channel. Surely, you're a little more likely to succeed today than you were yesterday. You can't quit today because you didn't quit yesterday and quitting today would be inconsistent given the progress you made. I once spent ten years trying to get a startup to work that clearly wasn't going to. And I'm just now finishing year one of another startup that will, in all likelihood, play out similarly.

Fines

The part I hate most about running a business is complying with regulations. I dread checking my mailbox because I'm constantly getting fined for shit. Once, I got fined $41,000 by the NYWCB, whatever that is, for not having Workers' Compensation Insurance, whatever *that* is. But after complaining to the department that I didn't *really* owe them that kind of cash and that, even if, suppose, I did owe it, I couldn't *really* afford it, I got the fine reduced to $1,000, and I went on my way. Another time, I was sent a bill for eighty grand in unpaid taxes. I assured them it was a clerical mistake. I got it updated to a tiny refund in my favor.

That's the story of fines. They're just scare tactics. If you have the courage to dispute them and ideally a sob story to go with it, they will mostly disappear. Finers bank on finees' unwillingness to fight, on their tendency to capitulate to ostensibly authoritative demands.

I think it's no accident that the word "fine" is named such. Because for the agencies who issue them, that's the absolute best-case scenario of how you'll respond:

"Fine…"

Socialism

When the barista asks me which country of origin I would like my espresso beans to come from, I pick the nation that I believe has the lowest per-capita gross domestic product.

"Single-origin Burundian, please, because, I assume, they need the GDP most."

Irrelevant Delta

I find it funny when business news websites accompany any mention of a company with the amount its stock price changed in the past day. Like, "Companies like Qualcomm (⇑4.18%) and Cisco (⇓0.04%) ..." Uh, I have zero idea what the price was yesterday, and even if I did, why does today's change matter to me at all? I say stick the market cap in those parentheses instead with no indication of its daily change. "ExxonMobil (XOM - $302B!!!) announced..."

More broadly, I'm a little annoyed that people in business and politics seem to be obsessed with changes and largely ignore levels. GDP went down by a quarter of a percent. Carbon levels are up 5.8%. The unemployment rate is down 8%. But, wait, what is its actual level? Isn't that even slightly relevant? "Apple is down two and a half percent today" could just as well be stated as "Apple is worth over 840 *billion* dollars. Still!"

It reminds me of that optical illusion where a dot in your periphery disappears from view if you don't look at it directly. As soon as the dot moves, you see it again. Clearly, something in our psychology is thoroughly bored by stasis and highly attuned to change.

> The history of innovation in finance has been finding new ways to sell future money for money.

Deadweight Loss

There's a concept in microeconomics called "Deadweight Loss." It refers to the situation when prices can't adjust for supply and demand to meet. For example, a government-mandated price ceiling that leads to shortages; or a monopoly situation that prevents competitors from offering the same product at a lower price. It's considered a "deadweight" loss because there are transactions that rational market participants would have liked to execute but are for some reason prevented from engaging in freely, thus leading to an unforced reduction in a nation's gross national product.

The point I would like to make is that, in my opinion, the purest form of Deadweight Loss is imposed on society by the forced practice of... matching socks.

No one wants to have to match their socks—I sure as hell don't—but as a people, we have decided to punish via ridicule those who don't conform to this social contract.

If instead, we were all to agree that it didn't matter, that mismatched socks is an admirable fashion statement, we'd save dozens of hours per person per year. If we could rid ourselves of this constraint, then we as Americans alone would gain over a billion people-hours per year. And those hours could be put toward more productive uses like, I don't know, building nuclear power plants.

Overpriced

You know when you're in the fancy part of town and you wander into some clothing store and you're like, *dude, that's a pretty cool t-shirt!*

You casually look at the price tag and it's...$240 plus tax.

You're like, *What the fuck? Are they out of their mind? That isn't worth anything close to that amount of money.* You storm out.

As an entrepreneur, I admit that this is how I feel about hiring my fellow Americans. Like who do you think you are telling me you need $140,000 a year plus benefits? Dude, I could get an entire village just outside Calcutta to spend 14 hours a day doing whatever the fuck I want for the price of your Brooklyn-bound-L-train ass.

Co-opted

There's a microeconomics concept that says: when a particular company in an industry uses a technology or tactic that improves their business economics, all other competitors must follow suit and adopt the profit-improving technology too. Otherwise, their margins will dwindle due to pricing pressure from the innovator and they'll be competed out of business.

When I watch political debates, especially within the primaries of a political party, I feel a similar force is at play. But instead of it being a new technology that must be adopted, it is an effective talking point that somebody utters first. If one candidate figures out it is politically advantageous for them to say, "I am fully in support of [insert populist idea here]," then many other candidates will realize the same, and say the same until all coincidentally hold the same populist positions.

Benevolent Liars

If a politician has pure motives and also realizes that none of those motives will matter unless she gets elected, that politician will be forced to lie. About her beliefs. About her plans. About her motivations.

So, let's not impugn the honesty of liars. They may just be working overtime to do good in the world.

> "NOW, THEREFORE..." is something you find in legal contracts. I propose modernizing that to "SO, LIKE..."

State Your Claim

I HATE WHEN politicians mix social policy with proclamations about microeconomics. They'll say things like, "Better paid employees mean happier employees, and that's just good business!"

Tell me, politician, what is it you're saying about paying employees better?

- It leads to increased shareholder value, but the company's finance team has not realized this.
- It is a moral imperative and companies should do it without regard to shareholder value.

Both are fair arguments to make! Either may be true! But they are different arguments.

In attempting to make both, politician, you've managed to make neither. And you've lost some of my coveted respect to boot.

College Subway Ads

The more "punny" college advertising is, the worse the school. Do they think we haven't figured out this correlation? Do they not realize their wordplay does them a disservice?

The institutions whose subway ad is "Next Stop: Your New Career" or whose freeway billboard is "Your MBA in the Fast Lane" is barely hanging onto their accreditation.

You're never going to see "MIT: Technically, Your Last Stop!" or "Stanford: All Aboard the Silicon Valley Express."

Gosh, sometimes I'm so pretentious.

he who makes light of addiction

ADDICTAPOLOGIST

Marijuana Addict

I pretty clearly have an addiction to marijuana. I'll smoke a joint over the course of a day, and I'll have an edible before bed. When I go a day without weed, I get irritable. I fail every time I decide to quit.

I tell myself that pot addiction isn't nearly as harmful as an addiction to opiates or even alcohol. Hell, I'm pretty sure pharmacology says it ain't even a real thing. But it is cool that I get to experience what addiction is like: the denial, the furtiveness, the dismissing as *not at all a problem.*

Indeed, I don't think it's a problem. I really don't. I credit weed for my creativity to the extent I have any. Yet, I would be mortified if how much I use was known by my friends and family. Deep down, I know it is a huge problem derailing my life and I'm too weak to fix it. How conflicting. And how reminiscent of the other cases of addiction I've witnessed.

To non-addicts, our compulsion seems utterly illogical and self-destructive. But to our own minds, it is mere maintenance of what it's used to.

From what I've read about addiction, it's a sort of rewiring of the brain. The brain gets used to a certain chemical being there and gets pissed at its truancy. Water quenches thirst, sleep relieves fatigue, and drugs rectify chemical deficiency.

Nausea

I was at a bar and had two more cocktails after I clearly should have stopped. I left, stopped by a taco truck, and ate the mushroom burrito I bought on my walk home. I got back to my apartment around 3 am, brushed my teeth, put on my Invisalign retainers, threw my clothes on the floor, and got in bed.

I looked at the ceiling. The room was spinning. My head was throbbing. I didn't feel quite right, and I thought, *I know I could fall asleep, but I also know I could vomit. I have the power to decide.*

So, out of respect for my tomorrow, I dragged myself back to the bathroom and knelt over the toilet bowl until I was successful at ejecting some toxins and their bystanders. Nice to see you again, *burrito con hongos*. I'll chew you better next time.

There was something about that moment that made me very self-conscious—my head in the toilet bowl, vomiting, staring at the food and drink I spent a fortune on, feeling terrible, not laughing anymore. *How did this happen? Have I no self-control? What would my parents think if they saw me in this state?*

And then, in what may have been either genuine bashfulness or a drunk attempt by my subconsciousness to lighten the mood, I was reminded who had front-row seats to this whole ordeal: my Invisaligns. I had this questionably serious thought about them:

I hope they're not judging me.

Side Effects Be Damned

Addiction is unavoidable. Even if you're committed to conventional sobriety, there are things you do that give your mind pleasure that you are powerless to stop doing them. Maybe it's a destructive relationship, maybe it's masturbation, maybe it's Talenti gelato. To an outsider, who just doesn't get it, your compulsion and lack of self-control is irrational, jeopardizing your health, wasting your time, not to mention your life.

But that's not a sentiment you can relate to. Because the thing you're addicted to is a thing you love doing and doing less of it sounds like the opposite of ideal.

> Meditation is a drug I won't try. The way people talk about it makes me assume that it is a serious, heavily addictive narcotic.

Self-Medi(c/t)ating

"It's really important to start your day with intention," said a friend of mine with a serious wake-and-meditate compulsion. His decline into ritual mindfulness had been sad to watch. What started as innocent breathwork progressed into harder practices. Just last summer, he went on a ten-day meditation retreat.

What's the point of meditation? Why is thoughtlessness some kind of ideal? I, for one, have lots of things to think about, and I'm constantly battling against the clock to get in sufficiently many thoughts each day. You're asking me to take time out of my day, to silence my mind, to switch off contemplation, to quiet the internal monologue, which is as close to a self as I can reasonably claim to have?

Yes, everyone says meditation is amazing. But everyone says cocaine is amazing too.

If we, as a society, were to advise adolescents on whether to experiment with mental relaxation, especially when it comes to that hard, transcendental stuff, we should counsel them to *just say no*.

Experiencing Vice

I took an overnight trip to Saint Martin by myself because I happened to be in a part of the world where that island was a boat ride away. The Caribbean isle is tiny, yet is claimed by two nations, France and The Netherlands. They apparently agreed to disagree by splitting the land protrusion in two.

I decided to stay on the French side because I had hoped to practice my French, which had been getting rusty since I graduated from a French immersion secondary school in Canada a decade prior. I chatted up a bartender at happy hour who mentioned that there were casinos on the Dutch side of the island. *Casinos.*

At the time, even as a 28-year-old, I had somehow never gambled at a casino. I took a taxi to the Dutch side and strolled through the doors of Casino Royale. The sights and sounds were intoxicating, the stench of cigarettes surprising. I sat down at a $5 blackjack table and put down $25, ready to make my first bet. I ordered a gin & lime, which arrived promptly and for free. A fellow gambler and the dealer taught me the basics of Blackjack, and within twenty minutes, I was splitting aces, doubling down and I quintupled my buy-in to $125! *Look at me go!*

But, I knew how casinos make their money, and I, for one, am not a sucker. So, I did the responsible thing and quit while I was ahead. I cashed in my chips, bid my new friends adieu, and strolled out of the casino a *nouveau riche*.

The glimmering lights of an apparent strip club across the street caught my eye. I was also inexperienced with such establishments and I had no other plan, so I went in.

There, I discovered that drink prices at strip clubs are out of control and the pressure from strippers to get a lap dance is bonkers. I, for one, am not one to give in to overpriced gimmicks.

So, I did the responsible thing. I finished my drink, wished the stripper I was talking to well, left the strip club, and went back to the casino to collect some more of their money and lap up some more of their free booze.

This time, I sat down at the Big Boy table: $25 minimum bet. *Fuck it*, I thought, *I'm up $100. I obviously have a knack for this game; what's the worst that could happen?*

Within a cool eight minutes, I lost my $125 plus another $300 I had withdrawn from the ATM trying to win my losses back, and the cocktail waitress never showed.

Holy shit, I thought, *I had better stop gambling.* So, I summoned the courage to do the responsible thing. I cut my losses, left the casino, and marched back to the strip club where I wouldn't be subjected to such highway robbery.

There, I was quickly reacquainted with the stripper who had been hounding me earlier to get a lap dance. Thirty dollars was the pitch. I had never gotten a lap dance before.

Fine, I rationalized, *that's a single hand of blackjack. I've got that remaining in my wallet.*

So, to the back room we went, and as promised, beautiful breasts made their appearance. *Oh look, now they're in my face.*

I was comfortably drunk by then, the music was loud, I had a stripper dancing *on* me, and my dour mood from the gambling loss was subsiding. *I could get used to this life,* I thought. I imagined myself growing old on this two-nation island, picking my French back up, stopping in at the strip club every once in a while.

The stripper leaned into my ear to say something I assumed would be *dirty*. "It has been four songs now," she said, "so, $120. you're having fun and want me to keep going, right?"

I was jolted from my trance.

"Wait, what? I thought you said the lap dance was thirty dollars!"

"Oh no," she said, "that's per song. It has been four songs now, and of course, a tip is appreciated here in Sint Maarten!"

I called an end to this madness and lied I didn't have the money. She put her clothes back on *posthaste* and summoned the strip club manager to handle the situation.

He, an imposing-looking fellow, informed me that the bill was non-negotiable and that if I didn't have cash, they accept all major credit cards. He also "trusts" that I don't want any problems tonight.

I somehow negotiated the bill to a more manageable $50, paid up, didn't tip, and got the hell out of there as fast as I could.

At that point, I knew I shouldn't go back to the casino because I was now supremely broke and I also knew shouldn't drink anymore because I was clearly not walking straight.

So, I did the responsible thing and bought marijuana from some guy off the street.

Fiction & Addiction

ADDICTION IS A problem in this country. Drug addiction is the one we hear about, but I'm not so quick to judge. Because what is addiction? It's the increasingly frequent doing of something you genuinely enjoy doing. So frequent can it become, though, that it can claim a significant portion of your time, health, money, and relationships, turning your brain into a fiend, thus being detrimental to your overall well-being.

I'd like to talk about an unspoken epidemic: fiction addiction.

I'm shocked at how cavalier people are about recommending a new TV series to watch. I have never seen Game of Thrones, The Office, Entourage, or any of those other dumbass series, not to mention sports and movies, that you fellow humans seem to love. People, *all the time*, will be like, "Dude, you haven't seen Game of Thrones? It's, like, *epic*!"

To which I say, "Dude! I think it's, like, *well documented* that people who watch an episode of that presumably mesmerizing series go on to watch the entire series, a full 60 hours of God-knows-what. When that's done, they'll crave another series to fill the void. If losing sixty, let alone six hundred, hours of my disposable time is the risk I take by experimenting with your series 'just once,' I'm going to pass. I'm a risk-seeking addiction-prone hedonist like the rest of you, but there are some vices even I can muster the strength to avoid."

More broadly, I declare fiction *in general* a complete waste. The problem with is right in the name: *fiction*. What a self-referential diss. What a defeatist attitude to a supposed form of art. Fiction, by definition, did not happen, will not happen, and rarely relates to something that *could* have happened. I know you forcefully disagree.

Fiction is, on the whole, contrived, overdramatic, vapid, pointless, and devoid of substance. Fiction offers no accurate insight into how the world works, and figuring out how the world works should be everyone's only goal, in my view.

I got a call from my cable company the other day. It was an agent who wanted to sell me a TV package because he noticed I didn't have one with my internet package.

"Hello sir," he began, "I wanted to tell you about some specials we have on TV packages. Would you be interested in that?"

"Nope," I said, aiming to shut him down right there.

"Aren't there TV shows you'd like to keep up with? We have some great deals on…"

"I said, 'No.'"

He redirected his line of inquiry. "And why is that? Don't you think it would be nice to watch some television shows in the evening after work? Maybe you'd like to keep up with your favorite sports team in your free time?"

I raised my voice. "For the third time, no!" Then, I went on a totally uncalled-for rant. "No, I don't want to watch some 'television in the evening' because I don't believe watching television is an appropriate use of time. Did you know that there is an awful famine going on in Africa in which twenty million people are without food and are perishing in great numbers? Did you know the carbon levels are rising at such an alarmingly fast rate that animal species are going extinct five thousand times faster than they were before we started burning everything that we could get our hands on? Wouldn't it be nice to think about those things when you come home from work in the evening? Shouldn't you want to keep up with those societal ills in your free time? Shouldn't you *personally* acknowledge your own role in this mess, peddling your visual crack to us educated New Yorkers who have the connections to make a difference, attempting to endear us would-be concerned citizens to your mindless, addictive, saccharine gunk which serves no other apparent purpose than to distract us from the literal burning of the world?? ...Hello???"

"Sorry, sir," he said with a Filipino accent, breaking the silence. "Please call us back when you will be interested in our TV packages."

juvenile math jokes

QUANTITITTY

Hundapacent

PEOPLE LOVE TO say "100%" to mean "yes" or "totally." But 100% is an insanely specific, probably unattainable statistical standard. Academic researchers spend entire careers in the quest of $p<0.05$, and you want to assert *100%* as if absolute certainty were not itself the subject of great debate? Chill out, dawg.

The surest I could ever be about anything is 98%. And I'd reserve that level of confidence for only the most tautological tautologies, like 2+2=4. Could I be misconceiving what addition is? Could I be actually insane unawares? Doubt it! But out of an abundance of caution, I give the chance I am, 2%.

I would love to be able to respond to someone who asks me if I'll come hang out later, "Yeah, man, 90%!" to express how certain I am about what I'm saying. But I'd get questioned. "Whatchoo mean 90%? Why you such an indecisive bitch?"

I admit I know the answer to my question of why people use *100%* when they mean "I'm pretty sure." It's because colloquial certainty is not statistical certainty. *100%* is an informal English slang that roughly translates to *88%* in *Probability*.

Always a Probability

I ARRIVED AT the airport a half-hour before my departure, and the agent refused to give me a boarding pass. Apparently, 45 minutes prior to boarding time is the hard stop at JFK. She said I could get on standby for the next flight.

Sigh. Okay.

As the agent was setting up my standby reservation, I asked her what she thought the probability of my making that flight would be.

She looked up at me and glared. "Sir, there is *always* a probability."

I was stunned.

Was she confusing the notion of *probability* for that of *possibility* and issuing a little snark to boot? Or was she making the offhand *astounding* claim that I, a one-time student of statistics, had never heard before? —that probability itself is eternal, that after I do or don't make that flight, the probability that I would have made the flight will remain immutable for all of time.

I contemplated this during the six hours I had to wait until I found out that I did not, in fact, make the flight. But, thanks to her, I now believe there will always be a probability that I did.

Street Smart

I was walking down the street by myself, like a baller. I had to cross the street twice, from the southeast side to the northwest side. As I looked around, I noticed something cool: there were no cars coming from any direction. I said, "Yo homies, I'm 'bout to cross this street... diagonally." And I did that. Like a super baller.

But reaching the far corner felt anticlimactic. Had anyone realized what I had just done? Did anyone grasp the significance of that move? Could even I quantify the degree to which I had asserted dominance over my ambulatory peers?

Picture it: me, flouting crosswalks, engaging in extreme jaywalking, crossing the literal center of a New York City intersection where perhaps no man had gone on foot before. I was a legend among pedestrians. But how much so? The question nagged me.

And then it hit me. I had just traversed the hypotenuse of a right triangle.

For the first time in my adult life, I could finally invoke... the Pythagorean Theorem, $A^2+B^2=C^2$.

Mental calculus swirled in my head. If I assume the crosswalks are legs A & B of a single unit each in length, then the square of my diagonal path, C, must equal $1^2 + 1^2$! So, if C is the square root two, and I would have otherwise walked 2 full law-abiding units, I divide the former by the latter, getting 0.7071, the ratio of my steps to everyone else's! If I subtract that from one, I get 29.29%, the proportion of steps I saved!

"Please note!" I exclaimed to the world, making only a minor mathematical leap of faith. "I am nearly 30% extra baller!"

And *that*, kids, is when you'll use geometry when you're older.

Imprecision

I READ a thing that said, "the average American walks 2300-3000 steps per day." The sloth that conveys notwithstanding, I must say that people are so imprecise with how they characterize data. Is the average of 2 and 10, "5 to 7"? No, it's "6."

And when you say "Average American," do you mean "Americans, on average"? Or do you somehow mean the modal American, as in the most typical, cliché, "average," boring individual that inhabits this country? And when you use the term *average*, are you sure you don't mean *median*? And if you'd be so technical to use the word median yet still cite a range, then do you perhaps actually mean *interquartile range*?

Your lack of answers to my questions leads me to believe you're just making shit up. It makes me think you're mocking me. Your misuse of statistics borders on criminality. You ought to get a citation*.

* For those who don't get my brilliant double-entendre, a citation is both a bibliographic reference to a data source a document that formalizes a minor criminal infraction.

Q. How much bigger is 200 quintillion than 200,000 quadrillion? A: They're the same. I just thought I should remind you how orders of magnitude work.

Positive Negative EV

Gambling takes many forms. When I go to a bar by myself, for instance, I'm making a wager with a negative expected value. Most of the time, I'll stare at my phone. I'll spend more money than I should. I'll increase my likelihood of developing alcoholism.

But sometimes, in theory, I could meet the love of my life, I could hit it off with a future business partner, I could come to a realization that gives my life a purpose. All sorts of things *could* go right, and therein lies the conundrum.

I know I shouldn't go to the bar by myself in the same way that I know I shouldn't gamble or take drugs. The logic is clear: do it repeatedly, be a loser. But do it never, miss out on life's greatest hits.

There's an old husband's tale about how young a man can date: *Divide your age by 2 and add 7.* But, me, I use a different formula: *Multiply your age by 0, and add 18.*

RUOK?

THERE WAS a bomb that went off on W. 23rd St. about forty blocks from where I live. Twenty people were injured, and it was international news. Three family members texted me to make sure I was okay. Which surprised me.

I looked up some stats, and every day in New York City, around 240 people *die*, and I estimate some one million people will stub their toe. If you're going to text me to see if I was one of the twenty injured by that bomb, I expect you to frantically call me on a daily basis to see if I'm even alive anymore. I'll need you to send me monthly sympathy letters with condolences to my toe, which you know with near statistical certainty has sustained an injury of some kind in these past few weeks.

> The median is, like, never higher than the average. Left skewness is fabled. I am certain no one but me finds this to be a good joke.

Bit of Both

HERE'S WHAT people say when they're asked which of two plausible causes leads to an outcome: "Hmm, it's probably a bit of both!"

As if that adds anything to the discussion.

Nature or nurture? "Hmm, it's probably a bit of both." The humidity or the heat? "Probably a bit of both!!" Hard work or dumb luck? "Per my rigorous analysis, I can conclude that each of the two postulated dependent variables may be considered to be considered contributory factors!"

I could have told you it was a bit of both. My dead Shih Tzu could have told you it was a bit of both. What I'm obviously asking is, "which of these two factors is dominant in causing what we observe?"

Pick one and elaborate! Choose a side and defend it! Argue that this is a false choice!

But please, *please*, please don't suppose that mere citation of the well-known existence of multiple causation could ever be construed as a contribution to the conversation.

Base 10

THERE ARE MANY parts of life and society that we treat as having some origin in nature but actually came about because some long-dead guy said it was so.

The one that trips me up most was my apparently misguided belief that our tradition of counting in base 10 has some mathematically or naturally oriented basis. For those unfamiliar, *base 10* means that when we're counting after we get to 9, we add a digit to the left. If we counted in base 9, counting would be all like "…6,7,8,10,11,12…" Counting in base 3 from what we call 0 to what we call 15 would look like this: 0, 1, 2, 10, 11, 12, 20, 21, 22, 100, 101, 102, 110, 111, 112, 120.

But that looks bizarre to us because base 10 is so ingrained into our minds as being the only way in which to count. Base 10 came into popular use, it is believed, because humans have 10 fingers, which made it natural for them to count in blocks of 10.

But if we had 11 fingers, and used base 11, then what we call 121 would be written as a round 100, and the "100-meter" dash sprinters would be a bit more out of breath at the finish line.

Speaking of units of distance, I notice that those too are completely arbitrary in their size. A foot was the length of *some guy's foot*. A meter is one ten-millionth of the distance from the equator to the north pole. Huh? A mile,

5,280 of the aforementioned guy's foot, doesn't even pretend to have its origin in nature.

A year is 365-ish days because that's how long the earth takes to circumnavigate the heliosphere, a.k.a. go 'round the sun. But if we measured years based on Mercury's sun-circling periodicity, I'd be 135 at the time of this writing, and the birthday cake business would be absolutely booming.

For these reasons, I have trouble getting excited about "significant" birthdays, anniversaries, distances, and really, milestones of every kind. There's nothing special about turning 50, except that if you take the time since you exited the womb, counted the number of complete axial rotations Earth has made in that time, divided that by the number of axial rotations Earth completes to

Mercury Calendar Birthday Party

reach the same position in its orbit each year, then divided that by the number of fingers you have on one hand, then divided *that* by the number of fingers you have on *both* hands, you get the number 1. Fine, I guess that is somewhat cool in the way that $-e^{i\pi} = 1$ is cool, but not in any other way.

If anything, base 10 is decidedly *unnatural*. Computers talk to each other in binary (base 2) or hexadecimal (base 16). Clocks use bases 12 and 24. Musical time signatures are all over the place. Rock music uses base 4, Brubeck's "Take 5" is in 5, and ballads groove in base numero seis. Pretty much nothing but our counting and accounting conventions use base 10 given the choice. Base 10 feels like as natural a phenomenon as morning dew and but turns out to be what some guy who has been dead for millennia—*millennia!*—pulled out of his ass.

Or in a more likely scenario, counted on his phalanges.

incelic vitriol at the institutions of marriage & kids

ANTIPROGENITICS

> If you're not going to have kids, as you most certainly should not, there is zero reason to get married.

Marriage Dissidence

NOBODY invites me to weddings. Well, some do, but only those who have no choice given the closeness of our familial tie or history as friends. Because anyone who knows me well enough to potentially invite me to their wedding also knows I think marriage is a terrible idea, dare I say, a horrible scam. That's not one of my fringe opinions I keep secret.

I mean…how insecure do you have to be to give in to the practice of entering into a legal contract that ensures mutually destructive legal proceedings should either of you want to declare independence? That's all marriage is: the bilateral imposition of ruinous misery should either party dare to defect from the union.

> I suppose there's a reason it's called the nuclear family. Because once it unravels, there are no survivors. And that's by design.

The point here is that no one wants a Negative Nikhil pontificating at cocktail hour about what a sham and an unfortunate relic of antiquity this whole thing is. No one wants to feel in their peripheral vision the smug glare of the dateless bachelor in the fifth row as they recite To Have And To Hold.

No one needs a hater. *Not today, Nikhil.*

But in actuality, I am the perfect wedding guest! I'll drink the right amount. I'll chat up extended family. I'll play that annoying-as-shit game of *So, How Do You Know Eric and Michelle?* And I'd never bring a date lest she misconstrue this farce as being in our future. So, you'll only pay for one! Finally, rest assured that I'll shut my trap about my dissent of marriage. Not a peep about it.

Still, I get it. Inviting me to your wedding means you're paying a tidy sum to intoxicate a guest who is opposed on the most affected philosophical grounds to the biggest decision you might ever make.

And for most, that's just not worth having me save their date.

Best Friend... Forever?

I'm surprised to see people post on social media: "Can't wait to spend the rest of my life with my best friend!" and "Married my best friend today!"

Really?

I mean, think about it. Who was your actual best friend ten years ago? Do you, today, which you had committed, then, to being their best friend for life? I should hope not.

Is there something I'm missing that gives people confidence that who they want to marry today is who they'll want to be married to at twice their age?

Wedding Vows

I propose updating the standard wedding vows to the more-honest following:

I, Marsha, acknowledge you, Santiago, as whom I was dating at this socially marriageable age. We'll get bored of each other, the fights will never end, and infidelity is a foregone conclusion.

But word on the street is single parenthood is harder. So, with these cokeheads as witnesses, let's do this thing and relinquish our freedom together.

Independence

I plan to never get married or have children. Will I, at times, suffer crippling loneliness? Will I die alone with no one who cares for me by my side? Will I spend my eighties as a sad, old, childless man, who never truly experienced love, who hits on sprightly sixty-somethings in smoke-filled pool halls in Boca Raton? Will my obituary read "Nice Guy; Left No Legacy Tho!"?

Yes, probably all true.

But that all sounds like a small price to pay for freedom. A rock-bottom bargain if you ask me.

> I was asked if I like babies. My answer: I think people should really, *really* stop making them. But I can't help but like them once they are made.

Long-Winded Diss

IT'S PRETTY INSULTING to tell someone they were an accident—a pullout method gone wrong; a drunken hook-up followed by a failure to procure Plan B.

But can we acknowledge a statistic I came across? Forty percent of childbirths in America were the result of accidents. Forty percent! Look it up. That's true. That's a huge number of us who simply weren't ever intended to exist.

In fact, dear reader, if we consider our respective conceptions, there's a pretty good chance—a 64% chance—that among two people picked at random, at least one was an utter mistake, an altogether unwanted human being.

But given what my parents tell me about their lengthy, deliberate family planning process, I feel confident that the accident here…

…was you.

> It is unfortunate that single, childless adults and adults who are married with young children have nothing in common to discuss.

Hostage Situation

Do you ever notice who pressures you into having children? It's people who already have children. These people are pretty convincing, so I think most people buy what they're selling.

But I also feel like most people don't have the moral fortitude to say, look, let us contemplate an alternative possibility that you are suffering from a potent cocktail of cognitive dissonance and Stockholm syndrome. Your captor, a one-year-old, has caused you so much grief that your only response is to say nothing in the world has more worth to you. Parents themselves will admit it is true: once you have a child, you are beholden to it, your social life is cremated; there is no way out. Yet, these same people say they "love" these noise-making, finance-draining, poop-spewing individuals—and I quote— "more than anything."

To claim unconditional allegiance to a thing that once caused you great pain, fear and sleeplessness is the same psychological phenomenon as the transparent point of fraternity hazing and gang initiations. The process to join the club was so excruciatingly painful that you'd rather tell yourself the pain was well worth it than admit that this decision was poor judgment of colossal proportions.

So it goes with parents who make shit up to overcome their regret. Like what a joy it is. Like how life before children was effectively meaningless. Like how when their four-year-old wonders aloud where the moon goes during the day, true meaning is breathed into every fiber of their being.

ANTIPROGENITICS

Puh-leaze. We childless shouldn't fall for it. And I'll take it further: We should condemn parents for their promotion of parenthood. Not only are they biased and wrong, but they are also doing the world a strong disservice. If there's one thing the planet can't support, it's more people who live privileged first-world lives of excess like I know you do. We, as a species, need to stop producing them.

> Let's not glorify childbirth with congratulations. When a person or couple announces their pregnancy, we should say compassionately, "I forgive you."

> For a country that reveres the notion of freedom, Americans sure are committed to the institution of marriage.

> Adopt.

> I've had numerous women propose marriage to me. Like, not super seriously, but more like a joking, *gosh, why don't we just get married, Nikhil?* But I feel like a few of them would have been on the wedding invites the next day if I had been like: *You know what? Fuck yeah, let's get married.*

Let Freedom Ring

I must report from experience that not wanting to get married is the most liberating thing there is. Let's look at it theoretically. If you do deem it necessary to convince someone to agree to spend the rest of their lives with you, you're going to go out of your way to suppress the more objectionable aspects of who you are, of how you'd prefer to live your life. There is a lot about who we'd like to be as individuals that is fundamentally flawed vis-à-vis societal standards. And so, you shut that part of yourself up to get some of that sweet death-do-us-part action.

But if, like me, you have no desire to rope another person into a lifelong commitment to you, then you really can be yourself. You can explore who your authentic self is. You don't have to fix a single one of your flaws. And, ironically, that free spirit makes you most attractive of all.

the portion of the performance when we make eye contact

INTERMISSIONARY

And Now, A Word from Your Host

All right, quiet down everybody.

That's better. How we doing tonight?

You there, reading this series of lighthearted jokes and rants, are you on my side yet? Do you feel like I could mean no actual harm, and thus have utmost trust in whatever logical path I take you on?

I sure hope so because the remainder of this book is going to get darker, then darker. Jokes will become farther and fewer between.

The program will resume in 9 minutes. Your bathroom is over there to your left. There are light snacks and refreshments in your fridge.

Those for whom nature does not call and hunger does not pang may stick around for the entirely uninteresting recitation of the story of my life.

INTERMISSIONARY

Two-Page Memoir

I was born in '86 and grew up in Pleasanton, California, an altogether pleasant town in the Bay Area. An only child, I kept myself entertained with such things as magnets and water pumps. I was painfully quiet except with my nerd-skewing friends. Around them, I was an occasional jokester. I chose the snare drum to be my instrument in the fifth-grade concert band.

My parents decided to move to Canada when I was 10, and we settled in White Rock, BC, a beach town near Vancouver, where I joined a public-school French immersion program and got a drum set from a pawn shop. I joined a punk band as its drummer at 16. We did some studio recording.

I decided I wanted to live in America as an adult. I went to NYU to study "business" at Stern. Transplanted to NYC from suburbia, I became a changed man almost overnight. I became social, even flirty, but was and still am a shy guy. I got my first girlfriend. I applied to transfer to Penn, got in, transferred, got broken up with. I played drums in various campus groups, got my second girlfriend, and I tried creating my first web company; it got nowhere. Another breakup. I graduated in '08.

I got a job at a startup in NYC. Got back with my ex and moved in together. I worked at my job for a bit doing various data analyses using Excel and SQL, then took a similar job at Yelp in SF. Broke up again. After some 16 months, I quit that job to start an online legal services startup, Lawdingo. It got into a startup program called Y Combinator in 2013. I was the runt of the batch and zero investors wanted to invest after demo day.

I moved back to NYC, miraculously managed to raise $700k from some foreign investors. Ran out of money 1.5 years later. Tried every trick in the book to keep the company alive, which worked, sorta; that company still isn't dead. At one point, Forbes mag put me on one of those 30 under 30 lists for my efforts. I had a series of short-lived girlfriends, most of whom remain my good friends.

I tried doing stand-up comedy at open mics in New York with the goal of mumbling less. I vowed never to do the same set twice, which forced me to write out every notable thought I had.

For 1.5 years, I kept my business alive by illegally Airbnb'ing my studio apartment in New York several days a week and living at the Borgata in Atlantic City. After the fourth eviction threat, I put my stuff in storage and moved in with my parents who were then in Vancouver, Washington, near Portland. I started another company, Vessel.us, a home equity exchange that serves as a mortgage alternative. It's complicated and, um, pre-success, but is ostensibly my main focus now. A pandemic struck, I stayed with my parents longer, and I recently moved to Wilmington, Delaware, partly for business reasons, and back to my old tricks of renting my place on Airbnb to fund my businesses.

While my open mic standup career has slowed to once in a blue moon, for the past six years, my personal hobby continued to be writing out my thoughts in the format of bits. That habit, through some twists and turns, became what I'm now, in mid-2021, hitting publish on as this book.

Act III: Habanero: Conception of Reality

science-adjacent rambling by a non-scientist

HYPOTHESCIENT

Distant

THE OBSERVABLE universe is 900 million light-centuries wide. Light travels at 671 million miles per hour. The observable universe is either nearly or exactly 0% of the actual universe. It is postulated that there are 10^{500} universes. And you thought your commute to work was long.

Star-Struck *

Look at the stars. Realize that those photons have been travelling for 300 years *minimum* and are, frankly, disappointed that slamming into your retina is how their story ends.

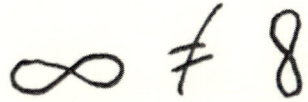

PEOPLE DON'T SEEM to care much about the question, is space *infinite or merely mind-bogglingly large?*

If space is infinitely large, then you can take the largest volume of space you could ever conceive of—say, four hundred nonillion times the size of the observable universe—and it will always be, by definition, precisely 0% of what's out there.

A finite and an infinite universe are such radically different scenarios. Yet the public's thirst to know whether space has boundaries is... shall we say, bounded. Even all the most cutting-edge research into this particular line of inquiry comes to the same, startling conclusion, "Fuck if I know."

But I must know. I demand to know. Is every person I've known, every sight I've seen, every bit of knowledge I possess some of what is out there? Or is it all a big, fat *zero* in the scheme of it all?

Gravity

Do you ever get stoned, go to a coffee shop to do some work, and look around at all the people smiling, talking, typing, sipping coffee, as if everything is fine, and think to yourself:

Guys, <u>guys</u>, how are you all not deeply concerned that scientists don't know what gravity is and if one day it decides to tender its resignation, we'll have ninety seconds, tops, before we are flung far into deep, empty space, left to freeze and suffocate, never having had the chance to say goodbye to everyone we love?

Okay, I, too, have not had that thought while stoned at a coffee shop.

> Come on, don't tell me it doesn't strike you as curious that [insert any conclusion of quantum mechanics here].

Dizzy

DO YOU KNOW, offhand, which way the world spins? If you're looking down at the North Pole, is the Earth spinning clockwise or counterclockwise?

Oh, you don't know which one of two ways you've been spinning round and round at a thousand miles an hour your whole life?

Well, you're a fucking idiot.

And so am I.

Fiery

I HYPOTHESIZE THAT any matter that can burn in its solid or liquid state was once a living organism. Find me a counterexample. You can't.

"Pure hydrogen?" you suggest.

Ugh, fine, pure hydrogen. Good one, smartass. Technically, H_2 can ignite and wasn't once alive. But find me *any* other counterexample. You can't!!!!

"Sulfur?" you offer.

Congrats, Niels Bohr. S_8 is flammable; matches are vegan; send my regards to your high horse. All I was saying is that most of the things you encounter that could conceivably burn—from perfume to linoleum—can burn because they got their burnable energy from a once-living organism!

"That's literally not what you said," you counter.

This is my book, not yours, so I say let's just move on.

Blackout History

PEOPLE WHO ENJOY telling their blackout stories after a night of heavy drinking remind me of the study of cosmology, archaeology, and history, but on a much smaller time scale.

Like, here we are living and there are these academics who are like, *yo, what the fuck happened? How did we get here?* It's the same way some frat boy tries to piece together his wild last night.

"Well, it started with a bang—six shots of Cuervo! —and from there, it starts to get a little hazy. There was some chaos, some collisions, some dark matter emanating from various black holes, some sex, some revolutions, and then, well, I woke up, and here I am."

> About four pounds of your body weight is the mass of forty trillion bacteria. By the way.

Uninformed

I DON'T KNOW how mirrors work. I don't know how light shines. I don't know how cells divide. I don't know how fans spin. I don't know how electricity flows. Upon reflection, I don't know how anything works. Yet, I get by.

Than Previously Thought

WHENEVER THERE IS NEWS related to science, astronomy, or really, research of any kind, the headline seems to always follow the format, *"[Noun]* is more *[adjective]* than previously thought."

As far as I can tell, scientists just start with some wildly inaccurate guesses—and God bless them because those guesses are way better than whatever you or I could have come have up with—that get slightly more accurate over time.

Slight increases in accuracy are big deals in science; they get their own press releases. How does news of such minuscule improvements in accuracy introduce itself to the world? Through a public humiliation of what had been previously thought.

Microkin

Humans and bacteria have a common ancestor.

In that sense, every day is a family reunion in which my distant relatives are sipping amino acid cocktails by the pool and catching up all over my skin.

I'll let out a hearty sneeze and exclaim, "So good to see you 1.8-trillionth cousin, *Lactobacillus casei!* Whatchoo been up to, Aunt 213 billion times removed, *Enterococcus faecium?*"

Genetic Code Transfer

Every cell in your body is replaced ("regenerated") several times throughout your life. Every day, in fact, 50 billion of your cells formally transition into the afterlife; may their memory be a blessing. So, the person you were is physically not the same person you are.

But how did your current cells get the info from their predecessors? You remember your childhood; your fingernails still grow. Clearly, each cell must somehow ensure its successor does as good of a job as it did, or else you would quite literally disintegrate.

I imagine the transfer of genetic code is like that awkward transition period when you're leaving a job and have to train the replacement they hired.

One aging corneal cell, a 15-year veteran of the Ocular department, books a conference room with the protégé. The elder cell begins his lesson plan.

"So, in this department, we produce mucus in the eye at night. I'm not sure why we do this, but it is what we do. As you're aware, my cell walls are about to disintegrate, and you'll be the big man in charge pretty soon. Just remember, every night, scavenge for gunk, and stick over there by his nose. All right, that about covers it. I'm going to go die now. Peace!"

Parallax

Parallax is the name of the phenomenon whereby when something is far away, it appears to be moving more slowly than something nearby moving at the same speed. It's one of those phenomena that make perfect intuitive sense but very little logical sense. Or vice versa; I don't know.

A plane crossing the sky at 600 mph covers less space in your visual field per second than does an old granny walking by your porch at 1 mph and appears to be moving more slowly. That concept is obviously true, but it's hard to explain why.

I have nothing more to say on this matter.

Shun Contraception

Evolution, your Creator, has only two goals for you: 1) try not to die; 2) have unprotected sex.

"Please," it implores, "load up on carbs, lose the condom, and spread your damn seed!"

Of course, we modern humans in modern society have complex goals and sexual desires that diverge from the mere quest to procreate willy-nilly. You can rest assured that evolution disapproves of all of that.

Heat Vents

IT IS SAID that the energy that sustained the very first forms of life came from hydrothermal vents in the ocean's floor and not from the sun's radiation. That makes sense to me.

On land and in almost all of the sea, the energy that sustains life can be traced back to plant photosynthesis of the sun's tasty rays. Plants drink sunlight, some animals eat plants, and other animals eat plants and animals. The sun is the origin of virtually every unit of energy within life today.

But I bet my bottom dollar the sun had nothing to do with the origin of life itself.

Because, yo, the sun's only shining one-third of the day and only then on nice days, and only then on the outermost edge of the crust.

If you're the first form of life, trying to make a name for yourself as the literal first living thing, there's no way you simultaneously invented the world's first solar-powered caloric battery pack that lets you remain alive through the dark of night. If there was no food to eat, no cells in which to store energy, you'd die at sundown. And that would make a terrible start to the birth of civilization.

Obviously, the first forms of life needed a 'round-the-clock energy source to keep them alive, to get them in the mood to find other molecular clusters to date.

Heat vents... *check!*

Spoiler

SCIENCE, UNFORTUNATELY, has all the answers. If you find some aspect of the world mystical, science will be there, with smugness, to burst your bubble. "Just dig deeper," it condescends. "There's nothing magical, let alone interesting, about what you're marveling at."

What Is?

It's unfortunate that when you want to get to the bottom of how something works, eventually you get beyond physics and into philosophy.

How does a true random number generator work? Well, it might observe a naturally random physical phenomenon like the position of a photon and convert that random noise to a numeric value. But was the photon's position random in the sense that it could have been otherwise? Or was it deterministic yet unknowable to observers?

Physics, in all its glory, must sometimes defer to philosophy. Regrettably.

philosophy of sleep

SOMNETICS

> One out of every three minutes of your day, you're asleep. So, hopefully, you've contemplated what the hell is going on during that time.

Sunk Cost

There are those moments you are trying so hard to sleep but can't. It has been hours since you started trying. You get distracted by your phone; the light it emits wakes you up further. You wish you had just gotten up and done something productive. But you didn't. Should you do so now? No, you're trying to sleep! But should you have, in retrospect, gotten up two hours ago and read a book or done some pushups? Yes. But you didn't then, thus you shouldn't now—just to maintain consistency.

It reminds me of when you're waiting for a city bus or train and it hasn't arrived for 30 minutes, and you don't know when it will arrive. Would you have walked or hailed a cab knowing what you know now? Yes. But you didn't. And now, surely each passing moment means the light from the arriving train is more likely to come into view in the next second than it was in the previous second. So, you continue waiting and hoping until the sun rises and you join the early morning commuters.

Oscar-Worthy

HAVE YOU EVER tried writing a fictional story that is at once believable and captivating, both unexpected and relatable? That's damn near impossible for anyone but the literary greats.

You and I, though, have a mutual friend who is embarrassingly good at this craft, someone we've known since childhood who can literally compose fictional masterpieces in their sleep. You ask, *who is this gifted, prolific storyteller with whom both of us go way back?* The dream states of our minds.

I am, on occasion, so fascinated by the narrative quality of my dreams. There's drama, conflict, romance, irony, comedy. Supporting roles played by people I hadn't thought about in years. Plot twists! Romantic revelations! My own brain is composing the damn story as it unfolds, and yet, even *I* am shocked to find out what happens next.

> Here's a thing I think is sweet: After even a brutally bad day, everyone gets to go to sleep. And for a time, they get to forget their problems.

Logical Lulling

Sometimes, I'll go on long mental journeys.

I'll be thinking about one thing, I'll find some logical conclusion of that one thing, and then I'll exclaim to myself: *well, if that one thing is true, then certainly this other thing must also be true!* And then I'll start thinking about that other thing, which will lead me to that other thing. And eventually, I'll fall asleep.

That's my idea of an evening well spent.

> Pillows must think all we do is sleep.

> I have little confidence that anything my brain tells itself is true.

Dreams or Lies?

PEOPLE LOVE TELLING others about their dreams, but no one wants to hear it. Dreams are fanciful and immaterial. They're stories that did not happen. They contain none of the introspective weight some claim they do. So, why burden others with the absurdity of what you dreamt? Keep that shit to yourself.

With that said, I would like to tell you about a dream I had.

So, in this dream, I'm on a plane, flying to San Francisco. As the plane enters the Bay Area's airspace, but well before reaching SFO, the plane starts flying low to the ground, which begins to concern me. I look around and others on the plane don't seem bothered, so I'm given comfort that there must be no danger.

Eventually, though, the plane gets so low that it lands on the freeway, taxiing down Interstate 5 six times faster than the next fastest vehicle. The drivers on the freeway swerve out of the way but continue onward. None are stricken. I look away from the window back to my fellow passengers to take some comfort in shared horror, but I find that they all remain nonchalant as if this were standard protocol for touchdown.

Then, I notice the plane is fast approaching the Golden Gate Bridge. The plane's wingspan is far wider than the bridge, and the wings will be snapped off within seconds. We'll likely explode into a ball of fire and plummet off the world-famous bridge to our certain deaths. Now, I feel genuine terror for my life. I feel it in my stomach. I look around the plane again, but now people seem almost bored, checking their phones, sending texts, adjusting the time on their mechanical watches. They look out the window, see what I see, and then look back at their phones. *What the fuck is happening?*

As we are seconds away from the bridge, I brace for impact. And…the pillars and steel cables of the bridge all expand outward such that the plane fits right through. Streetlights, pavement, and semi-trucks all bend out of the way, almost choreographically, at the exact right moment to let the plane proceed.

My terror subsides momentarily but is replaced with confusion. Why *would* the plane land on the freeway? How *could* the bridge warp to let a plane enter? Why *are* none of my fellow passengers even the slightest bit disoriented? How *am* I still alive?? A menacing alarm sounds. What *is* that noise??

I opened my eyes. I looked up at the unfamiliar ceiling of a hotel forgot I was staying at. And for a solid eight seconds afterward, now awake, I still had that feeling of dread. The discomfort of befuddlement. I was still trying to piece together how space bent like that, why everyone was seemingly unfazed, what will happen when the laws of physics regain their grip on reality.

Then, at once, the answer to every single one of these questions became comically apparent to me. All of it made *complete* sense, given one truth I had thus far failed to consider.

It was a dream.

Just a dream.

Oh.

The fear drained from me and the memory of the dream faded. I silenced my alarm clock, got out of bed, and went about my day.

Like nothing happened last night.

Like *nothing* happened last night.

Which should be surprising.

It should be surprising because I just caught my brain in a lie and proceeded to place blind trust in it for the rest of the day.

It's a nightly ritual I go through and that you do, too. We recognize and ignore the evidence of dishonesty by the organ we trust most and pretend that this same organ becomes a conscientious truth-teller the minute we wake from a rest.

Ladies! If your man comes home at 5AM, whiskey on his breath, lipstick on his neck, glitter on his chest, shirt inside out, and insists he was held up at work, you dump his sorry, lyin', cheatin' ass, and never talk to him again.

But somehow, that isn't the relationship we have with our brains. Dreams, a.k.a. lies, are exhibits A-Z in dishonesty. And if we're observant, we'll notice its fibs during the waking hours. See: psychological biases and optical illusions.

And, yet, again, we rarely consider our minds fundamentally dishonest.

Because, sadly, we are our brains and it's never fun to self-criticize.

Coughing Involuntarily

I MET A WOMAN at a networking event. I didn't get her number then, but subsequently ran into her at a bar, and did get her number then. Some weeks later, we went to a party together and ended up back at her place. We smoked a joint, talked about this and that, made out for a short while, and then she fell asleep with me awake at her side. I tried in vain to have her gentle snore lull me to sleep.

She coughed.

"Hey," I whispered, assuming she had awoken, but she had not. Her snore continued in the very next breath. That got my stoned self thinking.

Most of the actions in the human body are involuntary: the beating of your heart, cells' absorption of nutrients, the growth of your fingernails, the 3D printing of 1,500 sperm per second. We aren't able to will those functions to behave one way or another; they happen despite us. But plenty of other actions are considered voluntary like scratching your face, writing a book, choosing a movie to watch, and, I would have assumed, coughing.

But there I was, witnessing a woman cough in her sleep, which looked pretty damn involuntary to me. I'd go so far as to say anything you do while you're asleep is involuntary by definition. Can you hold your breath or snap your fingers while sleeping? I sure can't. Can you will yourself to have REM while you're awake? Not I.

If she was indeed asleep and performed a nonetheless, then surely I must reevaluate a lot. What if some of the things I had assumed to be of my own free choice are actually uncontrollable reflexes? What if those moments that we'd describe as being "quick reflexes"—say, catching something that is about to fall—are indeed *actual reflexes* in the same way a literal knee jerk is?

When I scratch an itch without deciding to, when I swallow food without giving it thought—can I really call those actions voluntary? Might those actions bypass whatever decision filter I have and get executed, myself unawares?

If I identified an action that I had assumed to be voluntary—that is, a cough—but could plausibly be involuntary, and if I find it believable that some other voluntary actions I take are involuntary, then I must ask the *big kahuna* of a question: Could it be the case that *all* my actions are involuntary? Every single one? Could everything, literally everything, we do be nothing more than an unstoppable series of uncontrollable reflexes that we observe happening and confuse for free will? Could everything our bodies do—from sweating profusely to clapping during an applause break to playing a rare tympani solo to getting dressed in the morning— not really be of our own volition in the same way a sleeping cough is not either?

Eventually, these meandering thoughts led me to sleep, but I did hold on to the question. And I did a bit of research in the following weeks.

As it turns out, my theory wasn't original. It seems to be the working theory of most neuroscientists. From the bit I've gathered about the consensus in neuroscience, a human's mind talks to itself like a squirrel's does, like a tree's does, like a bacterium's does. It does not consult with any non-reflexive external superego.

Yes, thoughts and complex reasoning transpire as did mine in that bed. But it's not possible to pinpoint a part of the brain that issues commands and forms opinions independent of the deterministic processes that are our nervous system. Yes, you have a definite sense that you are deciding for yourself. But brain scans reveal that decisions are made during brain activity that transpired significantly earlier than when people claim was the moment they "made" a decision. So, "deciding" is really "realizing what has been decided by a chain reaction" and "doing" is "observing what is being done."

Maybe *you* exist in earnest; maybe *you* have the power to decide. If so, I congratulate you on that. It must be a great honor and privilege! However, I admit I believe the neuroscientists who understand that lives from the microbial to the mammalian are all like wind-up toys, like elaborate Rube Goldberg machines, faithfully producing a chain reaction of electrical signals, chemical secretions, muscle contractions, information encoding and retrieval, etcetera, the result of which, I have to conclude, is the beautiful little delusion we call life.

thinking about thinking about thinking

METAMETACOGNITION

METAMETACOGNITION

Psychology Theory of Everything

WHEN I WAS in college, I claimed to have invented a Psychology Theory of Everything—a framework so comprehensive that it would reconcile every principle of psychology from the bystander effect to the paradox of choice to the confirmation bias into a single elegant model.

Here's the theory: People avoid doing what they believe others would perceive as the result of an arbitrary decision. By arbitrary decision, I mean a choice selected without clear reason from among a pool of options that all look rather similar in appeal to an outside observer. If someone could exclaim, "that's so random!" in response to your action, my theory is that that's what you want to avoid.

What originally got me thinking about this was when, as a Penn student, I saw someone wearing a Penn sweatshirt in a random Bay Area suburb I was visiting. I felt compelled to say hi to that person then. *Because, wow!* Another Penn kid in this kind of random town here on the west coast. But then, the thought occurred to me, if I had seen that same person wearing that same sweatshirt on Penn's campus or even in midtown Manhattan, I obviously wouldn't accost them with a greeting. I think most people can relate to this kind of situation.

What is it about seeing a fellow fish out of water that makes us want to bond, I wondered? And what is it about seeing fish in a sea of fish that makes us afraid to choose any one fish at all?

If the population of people among whom to say "hi" is one, and I do say hi to that person, then that's not arbitrary at all. But if they're one among many, and I've approached them at random, then I must explain myself. That is our collective fear and, I dare say, the driving force behind everything we do and decide.

I think people choose careers that their parents chose or that their friends choose because picking from the countless other possible jobs would be ultimately...arbitrary and thus more plausibly incorrect. You know how when you give someone a non-standard time ("What time should we meet?" "How's 4:41PM?") they say, "That's oddly specific!" In the scheme of things, 4:41 is as arbitrary as 5PM on the dot; I don't owe you an ounce of conformity to the blessed land of non-arbitrary decisions.

Anyway, maybe give my theory some thought. I do feel there's something there, something generalizable with regards to human psychology and I haven't read a single Psych principle that addresses this specifically as a potentially unifying theme among many principles that have been studied.

Forgetting

Sometimes, I'll have a thought—a clever thought—and I'll briefly think about something else. Then I'll come back to my original thought only to find that it's no longer there.

And the entirety of everything I know and remember will give me a blank stare like, "What?"

My original thought is clearly in there somewhere.

So, I say cordially to the organ upstairs, "Uh, Brain, heyyy, what was that thought I just had?"

Nothing. Continued defiant staring.

"Um, short-term memory? Prefrontal cortex? Just following up here. Would you do me a solid and recall that thought I just had?"

Pin. Drop. Silence.

After a tense silent standoff, my brain speaks up with an air of hostility. "*Really?* You want *my* help? You think I owe you a fucking favor? Dude, you pounded multiple shots of liquor and smoked a blunt last night. You think that doesn't affect me? What were you thinking getting my reward system hooked on gambling? Now, it's all I can think about! You think I can do my job when the cells that comprise me are being assailed by your unhealthy ways? Fuck you and your stupid ideas, man. I ain't tellin' you what you were thinking!"

I'm taken aback. But meet fire with fire, right?

METAMETACOGNITION

So, I say, "Brain, *Brain*, my dude, chill out, would you? You seem to have forgotten that *I'm* the one still paying back our student loans. I'm the guy who labored through problem sets, who learned interesting vocabulary, who got us a job, who took the risk of being an entrepreneur, who learned the art of drumming, who painstakingly taught you the arts of writing, analysis, wit!" My rhetorical gloves come off. "You'd be nothing without me, brain! Don't be insubordinate, you little shit; help your master out, and *tell me what I was just thinking*! This is my command!!"

My brain stays silent for a moment and then speaks up.

"Thank you for your request," it states, giving me hope of retrieving my lost idea. Then, in an exaggerated, mocking, staccato, robot voice, it announces, "Processing Command. Accessing Memory. Retrieving Brilliant Thought... Procuring Perfect Words...Considering If He Takes Credit For *My* Brilliant Work...Deciding If I Care In The Slightest About This Fucking Asshole... *Bleep, Bleep, Bloop, Bloop, Bleep... NAH.*"

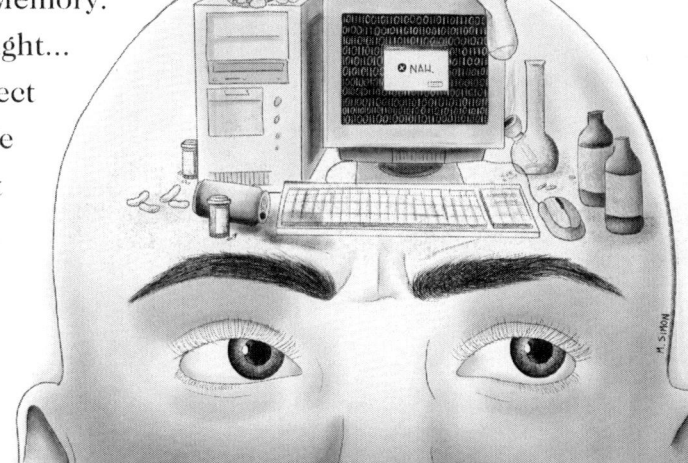

Telekinesis

I CAN MOVE OBJECTS WITH MY MIND.

Oh, you don't believe me?

Well, I can prove it.

Look at the title of this essay. *Telekinesis.* Now commit that word to memory.

Where is memory stored? Locally or in the cloud? Clearly, locally. To the extent that you remember anything, it's because a whole bunch of atoms inside your head changed positions in such a way that aspects of a stimulus can be recalled at a later date.

Now recall the title of this essay.

By making you commit a word to memory, I moved objects with my mind.

If that isn't telekinesis, I don't know what is.

4.8 Eyes

People who wear glasses are stereotyped as being bookish and smart. My theory is that this is correct. Poor eyesight puts strain on the brain, and strain on any muscle makes it a little stronger every day.

My own vision is perfect. Regrettably.

> The feeling when you lie on the grass looking up at the sky and see moving clouds, but feel you're on a boat sailing past a stationary troposphere.

> Why does anyone do anything? Out of habit mostly.

Mental Connections

Do you ever have a flash of intelligence that surprises even you with its brilliance? What's usually remarkable about those moments is not how complex the thought is, but rather how obvious and simple, in hindsight, the conclusion is.

That leads me to wonder: First, why can't I constantly have pure clarity on everything? And second, what does clarity even mean? What is it that fogs our minds, that prevents us from consistently taking in information, assigning it to the correct mental model, and effortlessly deducing what's retrospectively obvious? The answer is so close to the tip of my tongue that I can taste it. But it's just not coming to me now.

Cognitive Puppy

My brain is like a little puppy with its unproductive impulses. It's always like, "Can we do this? Can we do that?" "Niiiik, can I get some drugs?" "Nikhil, hook me up with some candy!" "Yooo, let me hump that leg!" "But first, a nap!!!"

There is some notion of a self that feels distinct from my brain. It's the guy who understands how I am to behave in society, how to at least attempt to accomplish my goals. But my brain is an overeager Shih Tzu who hates bathing, loves sleeping, and is most satisfied when he has accomplished nothing all day.

Internal Thought Police

Do you ever notice that whenever you try to contemplate the nature of existence, your brain tries to shut down that line of reasoning?

Go ahead. Try to think about what it means to be a thought-producing organism. Try to identify the exact origin of anything you think or feel. Try to ascertain what a thought or feeling even is. See how far you get.

Where do thoughts come from? Where do they go? If emotion is chemically driven, then what does it mean to be sad? It is nothing in words.

"Nope!!" says your brain. "We're not going there! Let's think about something else! Anything else!" And the subject is hastily changed.

Brains pull out all the stops to get us to steer clear of metacognition, to avoid existential thinking, to ignore the wealth of evidence that says consciousness is an illusion, not an actual thing.

Belief in existence is the religion of our times. Highly believable. Socially requisite. And false.

Inside Inside Joke

Do you ever catch your brain smiling to itself? Your brain does not let an inside joke it has with itself appear on your face, yet it privately processes the comedy of an idea it finds amusing.

Where Is You?

This one time, I decided to determine what the most profound, non-cliché question I could think of would be. I'll spare you the nomination process and the runners-up, but I will share the question that emerged victorious: *Where is you?*

Now, that question is not to be confused with, "Where are you?" You're obviously right over there, reading whatever this is. Sup.

But *where*, I ask, *where* in your body, does *you* exist? *Where is you?* That is the question. And how profound indeed.

I'll turn the question inward. Where do *I* deem to be the sites of the essence of my being? My head? My bones? My legs? My toes? Well, let me think about that for a second. And why don't you think about it as well?

[break for contemplation]

And we're back. All right, I feel *I* exists in my brain, in my chest, stomach, face, and spine. But I don't feel *I* in my fingers, calves, bones, skin, or…

Whoa, hold up. I have a suspicion as to why this might be. Let me Google something real quick.

[pause for Nikhil's research]

Okay, yo. Get this. I just looked up where in the body *neurons* exist. Neurons live in your brain, obviously, but also in your internal organs, neck, and spine. But neurons don't really hang in your shoulders, toes, or nostrils. Not in your thighs, palms, or bones!

Thinking is a process of neurons firing. And what are we but the thoughts we produce?

It is telling that we routinely use exactly the body parts where neurons are to describe our feelings, thoughts, and emotions. It was a *gut* decision. Use your *head*. She has a tough *spine*. That was spoken from the *heart*. Neurons are in all those places.

And thus, I conclude, so is you.

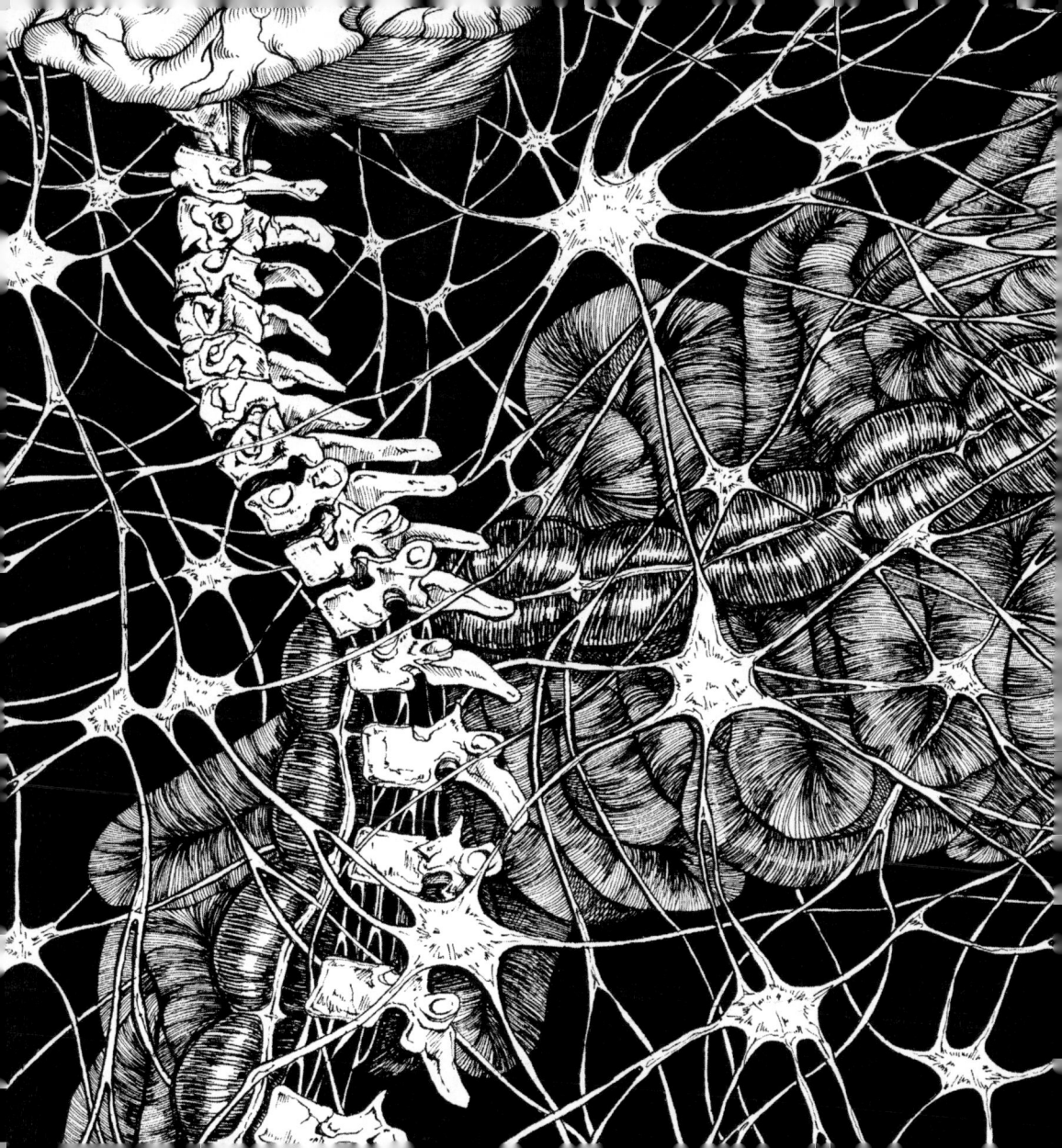

the minutiae of existence

EXISTENTIA

Life and...?

What's the opposite of life? Some may say death. But life is a period of time; death is a moment. Saying life and death are opposites is like saying the opposite of light is turning off the lights. No, the opposite of light is darkness.

People use the expression, "it's a matter of life and death." But that phrase strikes me as incorrect, as faulty parallelism, so to speak. Life and death are non-antonymous.

Some people think it's unfathomable that you stop existing when you die. Surely, there's an afterlife, they say. Surely, it can't just end, they say. And I concede there *is* an afterlife. And I will reveal its exact nature to you now.

The afterlife is equivalent to the before-life.

Remember what your life was like in the year 1861 and at the turn of the century in 4.7210883 billion BC? I do! My life wasn't like anything then because my life didn't exist then. Same deal after you're gone.

So, update the expression. It's not a matter of life and death. It's a matter of life and truly eternal nothingness. Or, at least, the early onset thereof.

… EXISTENTIA …

Solipsism

DO YOU EVER question the existence of everyone except yourself? Solipsism, I think that that silly, silly belief is called. Obviously, that's not true. I assure you I exist.

<small>Psst, hey, you. Yes, you. I have something to tell you. The rest of us are holographic actors in your life. Solipsism is real in your case alone. We're not supposed to tell you this. But I'm letting you in on the secret. I'm not real, your mom isn't real, your present crush isn't real. Existence and consciousness exist in just one person's mind: yours. We're figments of your imagination, extras in this lifelong dream you're having. If you don't believe me, try disproving it. You will be unable. Ask your friends and family if they genuinely exist, and notice how they glitch and fail to give you a straight answer. This conversation never happened. Now exposed to oxygen, this ink will become invisible in twenty seconds and you will have no proof it was here at all, just like you have no proof that anyone you know is real.</small>

Buh in the cosmos

People really want intelligent life to exist elsewhere in the universe. We're like little kids hoping we'll get a baby sibling.

Involuntary

Q: WHAT DOES IT mean to believe you exist? Who or what is doing the believing? Who or what is doing the existing? Is it your physical being? The collection of deterministic neural impulses we call *thoughts*? The digestive system that keeps you energized?

A: It's no one. Existence is a cruel lie, not an actual thing.

If A Tree Falls

I UNDERWENT A SPIRALING existential crisis when I realized that when a tree falls in a forest and there is no one around, it might *not* make a sound.

Because where and what is sound? Is it in the air for our ears to hear objectively? Or is sound the silent vibrations of air pressure that get converted into audible "sound" in our minds? The former is what I had always assumed, but the latter made more sense when I considered it. If I trust that logic, then a falling tree with no one to hear it would make no sound at all. The falling tree sets in motion tightly banded, inaudible waves of air pressure that dissipate like water ripples in a lake. If the waves happen to hit an eardrum before they lose their audible energy, the brain invents the sound. No brain? No sound. So I contend.

Once I reached that conclusion, the other pillars on which I based reality quickly came crumbling down too. What about color and sight? Is there really anything to see? Or are our minds converting invisible electromagnetic waves into a made-up visual field? What about touch? Is there actually anything to feel, or do untouchable subatomic particles whose mass mystically derives from a strong nuclear force and whose location is defined by probability waves get repelled by other such subatomic particles through some quantum electrodynamic force? Well, that actually we do know to be true.

If a tree doesn't make noise in an earless forest, then does anything exist at all? Is everything I know, including my "self" itself, a poor man's interpretation of virtually infinite invisible, inaudible, untouchable waves? If that is true, then what if there were no life? Would a universe that didn't have intelligent life to observe itself really exist at all? In what sense could it exist if it contained nothing that interpreted its innumerable sinusoidal waves as a fictitious reality? If perceivers disappeared, we would lose the last drop perception. And if perception disappeared, I have to conclude that for all practical purposes, we would lose our universe too.

I suspect the concept of reality somehow reduces to math and that there exists a quirk of mathematics that allows many or infinite spacetimes to exist. If there happens to be an observer in one of those spacetimes who can look around and "see," "hear," and "feel" the mathematical waves as light, sound, and matter, then awesome! —that means that the universe "exists" in the minds of those observers.

> Given plants and animals experience the universe differently than we do but experience it nonetheless, part of me worries that every time we let a species go extinct, we kill off an important version of our universe that existed.

And part of me worries further that if we let our own species go extinct, then the vast universe we see through our eyes and telescopes will disappear as well.

Those are some damn high stakes if we accidentally wipe out life on Earth and it doesn't exist elsewhere as I'm confident it does not. And, as stated, some damn quickly escalating existential crises arising from a children's riddle.

Virtual Reality

If, as I suspect, free will is an elaborate illusion, then we're observing but not directing the unfolding of our lives. So we're not the actors, not even the directors. At least we get to be the audience.

Forgiving

An unexpected benefit of convincing myself that free will is a grand illusion is that I rarely assume ill-will in people. They're slaves to chemical hormones; intent is not a thing; so, move on, and don't stress about it.

Identity Assignment

I FEEL UNSETTLINGLY FORTUNATE. Do you not?

There's this concept of identity, right? I can say that I am me. But why am I me? Why am I not you? Why am I not a diseased and orphaned child? Why am I not a penguin? Why am I not a bacterium chillin' inside a cricket?

Did you know that there are 50 birds alive for every human, 200,000 insects alive for every bird, and 500 billion bacteria alive for every insect?

I think most of my fellow atheists' working theory is that identities are randomly assigned to bodies at conception. I hereby name this theory *TRIA*: the *theory of random identity assignment.* I could have been born as someone or something else, the theory goes, but I wasn't. It was random. I'm me *by chance*. And what great fortune I had.

But I struggle to buy it. You're telling me that I lucked out to not only be born a human but to also have been born in America, to be happy and healthy, to have received a good education, to have lived in New York City, to get to work for myself, to drum and write as hobbies, to be living in the specific era that has high-speed Internet but has not yet suffered calamitous climate breakdown? You're telling me that my existence was dumb luck on the order of one in a decillion? It sounds very much like you take me for a fool.

But if not by chance, then how do identities and selves get paired? Why does my first-person perspective live in my particular neuronal network? Why do I experience eyesight through my own optical nerves?

———

There's a thing in logic called the *mediocrity principle* that says something like this: *You're most likely to choose the most common type of thing in a set.*

As an example: Suppose a bag has 99 blue marbles and 1 red marble. If you choose a marble at random, that marble is 99% likely to be blue.

———

So, if the mediocrity principle can be applied to conception, then surely you and I must have been born as bacteria, who so ridiculously outnumber humans in the bag of marbles that is our planet Earth. If we happened to get stupendously lucky, maybe we'll observe ourselves to have been born phytoplankton or, *inshallah*, roundworms. But existence as a mammal let alone a human would be far too much to ask.

Okay, on the count of three, let's, you and I, observe the type of being we ended up being. One. Two. Three.

Holy shit. I'm a human! Of the privileged and frequent-flying variety!
OMG, YOU TOO???

———

Given the mediocrity principle and our existence as well-off, educated adults, then TRIA can't really be true.

It's like those spam emails that say I'm the lucky winner of a one-in-a-million prize. *I'm not that gullible.* Delete.

Fear not. I have given this thought, and I have found that the answer to this most vexing existential conundrum is....

[drum roll, please, *brrrrrrrrrrrrrrrrrr*]

...above my pay grade.

I'm not actually a Plato-level philosopher.

Religious people, here's my tip to you: if you want to smash your sales quota and be the top-performing proselytizer, hammer us atheists with the dissonance we feel when we try to hold in our head the mediocrity principle and fact of our own existence. TRIA cannot exist in the middle.

Humiliate us with our failure to resolve this most fallacious fallacy infecting the foundation of our philosophies. Make us break down in tears. Deal us anxiety attacks. Crush us under the weight of our internal contradictions.

And, like the billions of existentially confounded souls that have preceded us, we, too, will bow down to God and thank Him for being our Lord, our Savior, our Creator, our Most Generous Nonrandom Identity Assigner.

TRIA-Solving Theories

All right, for real though, I have come up with two vague replacement theories for the previous essay's Theory of Random Identity Assignment.

One: intelligent beings are exceedingly more likely to have the capacity to observe their own identity, so the fact that we are intelligent is the only reason we're able to recognize our existence in our minds' mirror at all. In other words, 100% of beings that can contemplate their existence can contemplate their existence, which is a definition of intelligence, so if you're contemplating, you're intelligent.

Two: there isn't actually a distinction between identities. Life is the entire set of *autocatalytic reactions* (Google it) happening throughout the universe. Within that system are little pockets of information processing that are not directly linked to one another ("minds" as these pockets are colloquially called). The "identity" of the person who happens to have your "identity" is the "the self-recognizing" function being triggered in a mind ("yours") unbeknownst to other minds."

As I said, vague—nonsensical, even. But you try coming up with something more convincing because TRIA is straight-up false.

shining light on the expanse of time

TEMPORALUMINESCENCE

Time Scales

Life has been evolving for a while. Did you know there's a thing called a galactic year? It refers to the time it takes for our solar system to circle the center of our galaxy, the Milky Way. A galactic year is a bit longer than an Earth year; specifically, it's about 225 million Earth years long.

With this time scale, our universe is looking fi-i-ine at 61 galactic years of age. Our galaxy is almost as old at 60. And our solar system and planet are in their 19 and 18, respectively. The most primitive forms of life showed up 15 galactic years ago.

Then, eight galactic *hours* ago, the first human was born! What an adorable baby species! *Aww*, right? Aww.

Yet, in those eight precious hours of life, and more specifically in the most recent 20 galactic seconds after a trio of idiots introduced the internal combustion engine, Freon, and factory farming, we have managed to fuck things up so bad for our planet that our beloved Mother Nature, but a teenage mom herself, most certainly wishes in retrospect she had gotten that late-term abortion.

Because at the precocious rate were growing in population and vomiting CO_2, there's quite literally minimal hope, thanks to us, that mammals themselves will last more than another few galactic minutes.

TEMPORALUMINESCENCE

Recapitulating Prev. Essay

Life is aged 15. It had a bright future, but all of a sudden, it's terminally ill.

About 10 galactic seconds ago, it developed a rare form of cancer, modern humanity, which has already metastasized throughout its blood, bones, and tissue; through its land, water and air.

In 10 galactic seconds—the time it takes you to read this sentence relative to 15 years—this species has burned everything it can find to power the triple luxuries of keeping rooms at room temperature, eating meat, and being anywhere in the world by plane.

This has come at the low, low price of 50,000 species going extinct every year. Marine life? Suffocating. Terrestrial life? Burning. Avian life? Plummeting.

Yet, when we tune in to political debates where humans (life's cancer and self-anointed dictator) discuss how to best extricate themselves from this quicksandic quagmire they hath wrought, you find that they conclude that *two galactic seconds* into the future is deemed *far too abstract* a time horizon to consider when making decisions of life and truly eternal nothingness.

Or, at least, the early onset thereof.

Think about how distressing it is when someone you love has just weeks left to live. That's how sad I feel about intelligent life's present prognosis.

Time Traveling

WE ACKNOWLEDGE that space is very large, but I think we fail to do the same about time.

I have a question for you. What is the definition of *history*? Until recently, I thought history simply referred to the time before the present, basically a synonym for *the past*. But that turns out to be way, *way*, *__way__* incorrect.

The meaning of history, I learned, is the time before the present *about which we have a written record*. That amounts to some 5,000 years. Which rounds to 0% real fast when you compare it to the expanse of time that is *the past*.

The past, as most conservatively defined, is 13.8 billion years old. It's been that long since the plus-sized *Bang*. So, *history* amounts to a mere 0.000036% of *the past*, and, inversely, *the past* is 2.76 million *histories* long. The observable universe, for reference, is 880k Milky Ways wide. I declare time bigger than space.

When you want to study the time before history, you get into paleontology, the study of fossilized records. When you want to go further back, you get into astronomy, the study of how objects formed and moved around through space. And when you want to go further back still, you enter the fields of physics and its dumb cousin chemistry from whom you can hope to infer when and how all these elements formed and coalesced. Finally, if you want to examine time

TEMPORALUMINESCENCE

before time itself, I regret that I have to refer you to the Department of Philosophy because we just don't fucking know.

But what isn't under question is that human history is an insanely minor, cosmically irrelevant blip of time. Human history follows a stupefyingly vast duration in which humans had no role and precedes a much longer expanse in which humans will again have no role.

> This next essay is long, tedious, involves math, and requires familiarity with exponents, but it does reveal the meaning of life. I'd skip it if I were you.

In Exponentiation, I Trust

Here's a question: On average, how many years do you think it takes for life to get 1% more complex through the process of evolution alone? Be bold. Err on that shit being slow.

My own conservative estimate is one million years.

If that were true and life originated 4.5 billion years ago as we know it did, then there would have been the opportunity for life to increase in complexity by 1% an entire 4.5B/1M = 4,500 times. Could several thousand inconsequential single-percentage increases, if compounded, really transform the most primitive, microscopic life into modern animals among which are humans? On the surface, this seems so implausible that one can be forgiven for believing divine intervention played a part.

The notion of life originated when matter developed the trio of capacities of forming a membrane, converting energy into motion, and subdividing into distinct molecular clusters with similar internal processes.

Some of these molecular clusters randomly did "dumb" things like move away from sources of energy; and some, randomly, did "smart" things like move toward sources of energy. Some rarely subdivided; some subdivided like rabbits. Clearly, those that stayed alive longer and subdivided faster would become more numerous in population and would consume more of the finite sources of energy around.

Pretend with me for a moment that you are a third-party observer, watching this happen over the course of, say, 4.5 billion years. Collections of atoms stumble upon the conditions required for self-replicating. Self-contained molecular clusters exist and increase in complexity by 1% per one million years through the process of natural selection at the atomic level. You'd watch the phenomenon whereby the atomic structures that self-replicate more efficiently become ever more numerous.

After 100 million years of waiting, you find these microscopic, self-contained molecules are 1.01^{100} = 2.8 times as complex as they were in the beginning, barely a noticeable difference.

You wait another *billion* years. Now these cells are 1.01^{2000} = 439 million times more complex. They're clearly not alive in any conventional sense—specifically, they're now primitive single-cells, which, in fact, did take two billion years to develop. These organisms proactively seek sources of energy, they manage to store energy internally and they merge and mate with one another. But you would not call these sentient, conscious beings. They're chemical compounds reacting to stimuli algorithmically per the laws of physics and chemistry contained inside them.

You wait another billion years. Now life is 1.01^{3000} = 9.2 trillion times more complex than the first forms of life. And it's starting to get legit. You *still* need a microscope to see them, but you're seeing some legitimate multicellular germs now. Socializing, fraternizing, dividing into autonomous units, causing all kinds of trouble on the ocean's floor. They're still not conscious or self-aware. But still, what you see under the microscope has much advanced since the old days.

You take one more billion-year nap and check back in. Now, these guys are 1.01^{4000} = 190 quadrillion times more complex. At this point, their ability to detect and interact with light has become nuanced. They can distinguish violet from orange from pink. They're little sea creatures! You realize that these plus-sized organisms are the natural result of compounding complexity but that nothing is fundamentally different. They are responding to stimuli in complex but predictable ways and lack consciousness.

You take your final siesta and arrive at today, 4.5 billion years in the future from your first detection of life. Now, life takes the form of humans and delta-variants of coronaviruses and everything in between. These organisms' internal processes are now genuinely intriguing. They can now detect surface texture, they can recognize familiar "faces," they can distinguish between frequencies of air vibrations as "sound." Obviously, these randomly mutating membrane-encapsulated chemical compounds are *still* not categorically different from the randomly mutating chemical compounds of yesteryear; they're just the result of painfully slow, compounding growth in complexity. They still aren't "conscious," "self-aware," or "self-directed" any more than a cell is. But their information processing abilities are now absurdly advanced.

You learn that they refer to their own information processing as "thoughts," so you take the liberty of invading their privacy and listening in to such "thoughts." You find, to your great surprise, that these deterministic information processing organic units believe that there is meaning to their existence, that they are "conscious," "living," and "self-directed" in some different sense than the earliest non-living molecular clusters were. Almost all of them strongly disbelieve their existence is directly attributable to exponential growth in complexity of non-living chemical compounds and attribute it to some guy in the sky like, well, you.

Let's recap: We've established that the first forms of life were not alive in any way. We've established that they probably get more complex, even if very slowly, to the tune of 1% per million years. We've established that at that rate, in the amount of time "living" molecules have been around, they could have gotten 27 quintillion times more complex in their abilities. We think it's very believable that humans are around that amount more complex than the first forms of life. And we think that if you were an external observer watching this, you would find it amusing that these membrane-encapsulated multicellular think they're "alive." It is reasonable that you would find humor in these beings' confusion about the supposed meaning of life.

You would descend from the sky and say unto them:

"Hello, my children. Do you want to know the meaning of life?"

After tepid applause from the earthlings, you'd say, like a hacky performer, "I can't hear you!! I said, '*Do you want to know the one, the true, the <u>real</u> meaning of life!???*'"

Recognizing the significance of what is being offered to them, all of humanity would erupt into cheers.

And you would reveal to them the following:

"The meaning of life is that life can originate from decidedly non-living clumps of clay. Life is an obscure property of matter that allows molecules to band together, to convert a source of energy into movement, and to use that movement to find other molecular clusters with whom to mate. The purpose, the point, the one true reason for the existence of life is this...there isn't any; how could there be? Life is an accidental configuration of matter and human life is late-stage evolution—compound growth run amuck. To the extent you have a creator, She is but a triumvirate: random mutation, exponentiation, and time."

blasphemous rants of a devout atheist

RELIGIOPHOBIA

Secular OMG

I'D LIKE A SECULAR version of OMG. How about *MSMAA*? It would stand for *Maybe Something Matters, After All.*

You got the promotion!?? MSMAA!!!

It's a girl!?!? MSMAAAAAAAAA!!!!!

Irrefutabible

I WAS WAITING at a bus stop somewhere in Middle America.

Two older men were debating some topic; I paid them little attention. But then I overheard an argument that stopped me in my tracks: "Well, it's in the Bible, so it's true."

I looked up at the guy who said that to acknowledge his comedic gem. Then I looked at the other guy to see how he was managing to contain his laughter.

But all indications were that the first guy was completely serious, and the second guy had all but conceded his point of view in light of this revelation.

That was an interesting cultural experience for me.

Defeating ISIS

My strategy for defeating ISIS would be to fly twenty B-52 bombers over caliphates in Iraq and Syria and simultaneously detonate hundreds of... confetti bombs. It would be the most beautiful sight. And on each of the pieces of confetti paper I would have written in their native tongue:

THERE IS NO GOD.
YOU'RE BEING DUMB.

Blasphemy

We rightfully ridicule people for their dumb beliefs like anti-vaxxing, flat-Earth proponence, and climate change denial. Yet, we stay silent about people's religious beliefs, which, as much as it pains me to say it, are dumb. I can understand the appeal

Young children deserve better than to have instilled in them the fear of one or more supposedly temperamental Gods. Communities of people deserve better than to be persecuted for the spiritual lie they happen to have been told since birth. The future of the world deserves better than world leaders who claim an all-loving higher power will intervene to save us from self-obliterating.

We should be indiscriminate about which misguided beliefs we criticize and antagonize religion as the set of toxic, delusionary belief systems that it is.

You go first, though. Because I'm still afraid to ruffle pious feathers.

War on Christianity

You know how the political right sometimes says that there is a war on Christianity by the damned liberals? The liberals, of course, deny that, insisting they seek tolerance of all religions.

But I'm going to be the first member of the radical left to stick my neck out and say, you know what? I do declare war on Christianity. *In particular, Christianity.* Here's why.

I think all religion is completely moronic. America is 72% Christian, right? They have a commanding market share.

As a student of business initiation, I have been taught that if you're going to embark on entrepreneurship, you might as well dream big. Really big. I've heard someone say remark that Steve Jobs and a laundromat owner work about the same number of hours in a day. Steve just aimed higher with those hours.

So, in my quest to mass convert the populace to atheism, I'm going for gold.

If somehow, I single-handedly muzzled the entire religion of Islam, 0.8% of religious folk in America would renounce Allah. A pittance. If I snuffed the menorah of Judaism, 2.4% fewer Americans will show up to religious services. Weak! If I reached out to the Hindu community of which much of my family is a part and got them to abstain from their daily *pooja* to four-armed action figures, I'd accomplish just 0.7% less religion in my nation. Lame! Heck, if I got every single other religion out there from Taoism to Sikhism to Scientology and

Buddhism to shut their traps about their goddamn apocryphal deities, I'd produce a miserly 2.5% dent in American religiosity! What a waste of effort.

And what misguided rationale for war. If I really, *truly* want religion in America to go away, clearly, I have one target alone. So, die Christianity. I declare war on you. *On only you.*

10 Commandments

Given that we are all going to die and the life as we know it will cease to exist soon enough, the scary truth is that there is no objective basis for any moral belief you might have. You say it's wrong to kill? I ask why you think that. Could it be because you, yourself, don't want to be slain. And if people didn't think killing humans was an awful, awful thing, well then someone might just decide to kill you. But if that weren't the case, and you could unilaterally kill people without legal consequence or fear of retribution, let's be honest, it would be kind of nice in the same way it's nice that one can kill a menacing mosquito or appetizing animal without consequence.

So, what else do we consider morally wrong? Sexual violence? Animals do it. Evolution seems to encourage it. There's no law of physics suggesting it's de facto inappropriate. Racism? I will prove you're much worse than a racist in a few chapters. Adultery? Again, most animals are all about it. The only reason you're express *aghastion* is that you don't want me, specifically, to get your hot wife pregnant with my Indian babies. It is not objectively wrong to lie, cheat, steal, pummel or pillage. I'd be curious to hear you argue otherwise. You Kant.

So, given this default moral clusterfuck, what I think actually happened a couple thousand Earth years ago (note: 5 galactic minutes ago) is that some enterprising young man, let's call him Moses, recognized this problem, was disillusioned by the societal mayhem that prevailed, and took it upon himself to bring peace to the Middle East. He ascended a mountain, carrying a stone, a chisel, and a fat spliff in his backpack. He smoked the blunt to calm his nerves, took out his stone and began chiseling what he called, to his great amusement, *The Ten Commandments*. It would be an epic prank in which he would inscribe the objectively amoral (and not immoral) crimes he was sick of other people doing and ascribe it to the inventor of Earth he—*yo, crazy story!*—met while he was hiking, completely sober, *I'm telling you!*

"Rule number one," he began with a grin. "The name's God. Call me by my name. And y'all do what the fuck I say!"

"Rule number two, I am the only God. Any other similar claimant is a fake-ass bitch!"

That, by the way, reminds me of that classic restaurant sign that says, "Rule #1: the customer is always right. Rule #2: if the customer is wrong, see rule #1." Like, you were sort of going along with the first rule, but it's kind of annoying that there is a second rule preventing you from even questioning the first.

Moses starts getting of himself with these self-serving rules. He takes another hit, devolves into a frenzy of paranoia, and continued chiseling all of his deepest insecurities:

"Don't ever diss me, you hear?"

"Don't covet my shit!"

"Don't lie to my face!"

"Don't stab me in the back!

"Don't steal my bike!"

"Don't fuck my wife!"

"And God motherfucking damns it; I am *not* coming in to work on Sunday!"

Act IV:
Bhut Jolokia:
Permission of Death

vegan propaganda

VEGANISMISMS

Interspecies Equality

It feels like heresy to suggest the moral equivalence of species. I don't think I'm even allowed to go there.

To say that humans have no inherent superiority to cows is the hurtful accusation of animalism directed at all of humanity.

To liken the worth of hyenas to that of ticks is to deny the divine gift that are quadrupedal mammals in whom we see ourselves.

To suggest that barnacles and bacteria are evolutionary cousins is a truly offensive leap of faith that coldly assigns worth to a life form we massacre by the billions every time we brush our teeth.

To assert that single-celled organisms and sheetrock have a common ancestor in the cores of exploding stars is tantamount to the beyond-absurd argument that life is but an accidental configuration of matter.

In deference to decorum, I would never spew such hate as that.

"Don't be so preachy!" said the man who holds no true convictions.

Veganic Confidence

THERE'S A JOKE that goes, "How can you tell if someone is vegan? Well, they already told you!"

That joke is a fair criticism of us vegans. We insert our veganism into every conversation we can. We feel compelled to spread our moral stance to the world. Why wouldn't we? If you believe it's good to be vegan for ethical and environmental reasons, then it must be true that if you get one or two other people to also be vegan you will have doubled or tripled your impact.

At its most selfish, veganism is a personal preference, limited to one's self in judgment and ambition. But at its most pure, it's straight multi-level marketing. *Thou shalt convert*. That's the Vegan Doctrine.

So, I, too, can't help but proselytize upon meeting someone new.

"Hi, I'm Nikhil!" I'll say, extending my hand for a handshake. "I'm vegan! When I eat food, I choose not to inflict pain and suffering on the world. When I partake in mealtime, I'm uninvolved with rising methane levels. What's your name? Would I be right in assuming that you let your gastronomical predilection for cheese and chicken come between you and the pure nirvana that is a plant-based diet? It is just so nice to meet you!"

What an impactful way to save the world. And what an efficiently aggrandizing way to start any relationship.

> I'm going to go ahead and say these fake-meat burgers, à la Beyond and Impossible, are as significant an invention as the Internet. Am I kidding? I don't even know.

Milk & Eggs

Spend a few minutes reading about how milk is produced. Learn how cows are made to be pregnant so that their udders lactate. Learn what happens to the baby calves once the mother cow gives birth. Learn what is done to maximize the milk output per cow per day per square foot. Learn what retirement looks like for young cows who can't get pregnant anymore. Learn about the environmental effects of dairy farms and what culling refers to in egg production.

Then do what you want. But don't hide behind ignorance.

Juxtapose

WE CASUALLY display objects that contain all three types of matter: matter that was never alive, matter that was formerly alive, and matter that was alive and intelligent. Think: a mahogany-framed mirror with leather trims.

Old Age Meat

I'LL ADMIT I'M concerned about factory farms. Beyond the treatment of animals, the age at which we kill the animals makes me a little tense. As soon as there's enough meat on their bones, it's *off with their head*. And that turns out to be around the age of one.

Here's one, simple trick the meat industry could use to win back my business: Just sell me meat that died of old age. Natural causes!

Give me a cancer chicken sandwich and do serve it pink for the cure! The sudden infant death syndrome veal looks amazing; I'll have it as rare as the affliction that caused it!

But, please, keep your homicide wings off my fucking plate.

Death Row Dignity

Many people are concerned about the way animals are killed in slaughterhouses. I'm with them on that. It's brutal. Such killing methods, if perpetrated on humans, would be decried as war crimes, as cruel and unusual punishment.

In the spirit of offering suggestions instead of pointing fingers, I would like to put forth a proposal that I think all sides of the animal rights debate can get behind. I propose introducing to factory farms...*the electric chair*.

Now, hold on a minute. I can sense you're not on board.

"Gosh Nikhil," you say, "electrocution sounds a whole lot more expensive than a customary slash to the jugular. What's next? Due process? Courts of appeals?"

But come on, people! Cost should be no factor when it comes to preserving a modicum of dignity in our meat-producing ritual.

More to the point though, I suspect there's a marketable diet fad in here. Just like we have *grass-fed* and *free-range*, I think I may have invented the hottest steak label in town: *swiftly executed*.

I can picture it in Whole Foods now: a twenty-four-dollar pack of *swiftly executed* steak. On it, a photo of the actual cow you're buying, strapped into an electric chair, so you know it's *certified swift*. Wires affixed to all four udders. Hooves tightly shackled. A warden on call in case of disruption. A chaplain on-site at the herd's request.

Doing her best given the circumstances, the cow flashes a nervous smile for the camera as she is force-fed the last meal of her very own choosing: *hand-picked grass.*

Pet Food

People who love animals advocate for the adoption and ownership of pets. But what do they suppose each pet eats throughout their lives? Thousands of intelligent animals that are puréed into pet food.

Did you know the pet food industry accounts for 25% of *animal agriculture* and the resultant environmental damage? Did you know that *animal agriculture* is a blatant euphemism for the mass murder of mammals that are smarter than your puppy, more naturally social than your feline?

Animal rights activists, in my crazed opinion, should not be donating to animal shelters and advocating for pet adoption; quite the opposite. We should be arguing for the dramatic *lessening* of pet ownership in America and abroad; don't make me spell out what that looks like.

Now, listen a kid, my family had two cats and a dog. That dog was among my best friends. She got pregnant and had seven puppies, which was a cuteness overload. So, I get it. People love pets like their own children. No one wants to think of pets as environmental and ethical burdens.

But disasters they are, and I'm not wrong for bringing this problem up. Politicians never will, so they're mum about the issue. So allow *me*, with no political future to lose, to be the one to broach it.

And if you simply can't get over what a trash take this is, I would invite you to correct me if you're wrong.

Realization

Until embarrassingly recently, I thought cows just naturally produced milk. And I assumed male chickens had some role in egg production.

In case you've not gotten the memo, cows must be raped to get them to lactate, same with bulls to harvest their sperm. Cows produce milk when they are pregnant and for some time thereafter, just like other mammals. Because we enjoy dairy, we mass impregnate cattle.

Among the chicks that are hatched to be egg-making machines, all the male chicks are killed a day after hatching in by being placed in a gas chamber or tossed in a wood chipper. Their female counterparts are condemned to lives of misery.

Now, you *really* can't claim ignorance.

cynical analysis of the news media

MEDIAREALISM

News Reporters

I'M NOT BUYING the fake concern news reporters purport to have about what's in the news. There will be a report on a lion being killed in Africa, and the reporter will always be like, *Wow, what a tragedy that this happened. There are no words.* You'll never hear them say what I assume they actually think: *why the fuck are we talking about this? It's not even a person.*

I bet if you paid a reporter to report on some kid spraining his ankle, they would fall in line so fast feigning the most heartfelt grief:

Tonight, Sheboygan youngster, Jacob Stevens, missed a step and tumbled down two entire steps, landing the wrong way. Doctors say he may not walk without a slight limp for up to nine more days—just a stunning development. Sometimes, we all need to reflect on how precarious each step is, how debilitating ruptured tendons are. We'll be sure to update you on this heartbreaking situation. From all of us here at KTVU-Milwaukee, we have you and your family in our prayers tonight, Jake. All right, back to you, Cathy.

Like, shut the fuck up, new reporters. Ain't nobody think you care.

Sometimes, I'll see actual news anchors playing themselves in movies. I find that brazen. They're rubbing it in our faces that they are actually pretty good actors, that they can express outrage, sorrow, or elation on command.

News Addiction

The compulsion with which I check the news is alarming, even to me. If I don't kick this habit, I might accidentally spend a good chunk of my life keeping up with a series of inane, captivating conflicts that do me no good to know about.

> Reading the news often feels more voyeuristic than informative, not that I'm specifically complaining, as a fan of voyeurism.

Perennial

To save you some time, allow me to summarize today's news:

- SOMEONE IS UNDER FIRE FOR THEIR COMMENTS.
- THERE'S A TROUBLING TREND IN THE CLIMATE SYSTEM.
- A CELEBRITY DIED.

> News discusses what's new in the world. What's most urgent is usually not new, and what's not new is not discussed. People easily remain ignorant of the biggest tragedies in the world.

What the News Is

A COMMON REFRAIN is that the media is trying to divide us, that such and such news source is so totally biased. How about a more realistic assessment? That media outlets are businesses that get paid when people stick around for the advertisements or get addicted enough to pay for a subscription. What seems to captivate people is conflict, the more specific and personal, the better.

In other words, the media is in the entertainment business. If they don't think they're in the entertainment business, they will be outcompeted for ratings by organizations that do resign themselves to that depressing philosophy.

The media cares about neither the monumentally consequential nor the transparently trivial nor anything in between. They care about what keeps you glued to the screen during the commercial break or what gets you to fork over money to get past a paywall. That's their business model. If in today's news, a ship of eight hundred refugees sank leaving no survivors, and a celebrity threw dramatic shade at another celebrity, the latter wins the chyron because that's where the entertaining interpersonal conflict lies.

This isn't really a critique of the media but rather an observation of what people want out of any content. The human mind seems to be naturally drawn to sudden changes and personal disputes, not statistics and gradual trends. The brain just doesn't care about persistent plights that were here yesterday and will be here tomorrow. So, we don't get a special report on a famine in Somalia because we'd readily change the channel. *Booooorrringgg.*

If there is valid criticism of the media, it's *if* they purport to be in the investigative journalism business and not the entertainment business. It's *if* they profess to be the actual fourth estate, a veritable peer of the legislative branch, and not a functional sitcom. It's *if* they suggest that the reporting they put forth is an exclusive and exhaustive collection, albeit summarized, of all that is worthy of our concern. Such claims may well be an effective marketing tactic, a motivating rallying cry for the industry's underpaid cast and writers, or plausible deniability for lacking the moral high ground. But it's not what the market wants, and it's not what keeps them in business. It's also not fucking true.

All of this is unsurprising. Imagine a bunch of great apes in the jungle, who, over five million-odd years, very gradually became aware that there exists more to the world than just their local jungle, that their species is made up of more than their few local chest-thumping tribes. Then one day, these primates developed the ability to chisel the day's headlines into stone. And shortly thereafter, the hominids developed the capability of beaming any and all raw data and synthesized information to and from any corner of the Earth and beyond at the speed of light.

All of the world's deeply complex, often horrifying, rapidly changing information would become entirely available to these apes, all the time, all at once. Their brain biology couldn't possibly have had a chance to catch up. One might even forgive them for exclusively using this awesome technology for the purposes of voyeurism and entertainment.

That's obviously our story. So, we're still rapt by conflicts and metaphorical shit-slinging. We don't turn to the media to process the contributors to income inequality, the destabilization of marine ecology, the gradual spread of pestilence and desertification in far-away parts of the world. We don't instinctively care about such slow-moving, far-reaching trends because our minds never evolved to process or be stimulated by that. We go to the news to feel excitement and fear from the comfort of our homes, and we're given what we want.

That's our fault, maybe. That's the cerebral cortex's fault, maybe. That's evolution's fault, maybe. But you know whose fault it isn't? The media's. They're just trying to make it in show business.

um

NOTRACISTBUT

I'm not racist, but I don't trust hot sauce that is green. No one heard of a "hottest hot sauce" that was shamrock fucking green. *Salsa verde*, you'll never be *muy caliente*; this table is only for *rojas*.

Overheard in the West Village: one twenty-something white girl to another: "At that point, I didn't know what to do with my life, so I applied to grad school in China, I got in, I showed up, and I was like 'Ni hao, bitches!!'"

Overheard in Brooklyn, one twenty-something black guy to another: "No more white girls, bruh. I'm done with them!"

It's awkward when stereotypes are based in truth. Because stereotyping is condemned, but statistical inference is celebrated. What exactly is the difference?

Welcoming

SURELY, YOU'VE SEEN those signs at local establishments that read: "We welcome: All races, All religions, All orientations, All genders, All abilities. You are welcome here."

Listen, I'm down with the sign; I'm for the inclusivity. But I've noticed something about those signs that makes me question their intent.

Their existence appears to be confined to affluent, super-white neighborhoods, and nowhere else. A playhouse in Ashland, OR, a croissant shop in Park Slope, Brooklyn—you know, those kinds of places. You're just not going to see that sign at a Kwik Stop in Bumpass, Virginia, or at a Peking duck eatery in Flushing, Queens.

So, given the demographics of where, *and only where,* these signs seem to appear, I can't help but interpret the vibe they give off as defensive. It's as if they're worried that you might come to their store, look around at all the able-bodied, heterosexual, cisgendered, well-to-do, white folks and start to wonder, *might this place actually be turning away anyone with even the slightest hint of melanin or with even the most fleeting of bi-curious thoughts?*

"No!!" the sign preemptively barks. "We welcome everyone!"

Brown Privilege

I'M AN AMERICAN of Indian ethnicity. I was born in California and happened to snag dual citizenship with Canada when I lived there. My mom grew up in Delhi, and my ethnically Indian dad grew up in Miwani, Kenya. And let me tell you, I really feel like I won the gender-ethnicity-nationality lottery over here. As far as being a human goes, it doesn't get easier than being an American-born Indian male.

The vast advantages of being born both American and male are well-documented, and I won't cover them here.

But what's the deal with Indians? *I mean, what is the actual deal?* Well, we have delicious food, a spirit of innovation; a celebrated aptitude for math, science, and technology; and unparalleled wit. We're the most educated, highest-earning, longest-living, least divorce-prone. And guess what? There is no punchline! Being Indian in America is simply a delight.

It's like America forgot to be racist toward us. Maybe I lucked out, but I can count on zero fingers the number of times in my life I've personally been subjected to a racial slur or discriminatory practice. The worst I usually get is the incorrect but flattering assumption that I can code.

I'd say in America, Indians have it best. White people have it second best, what with their white privilege and all. But white folks at least get reminded to check their privilege on the regular. Brown is a privilege that has gone *wildly* unchecked.

For long enough.

Ahem. On behalf of Indians, in particular American-born ethnically Indian males living in large, liberal cities, I have something to say:

We feel left out. We want in on the societal resentment. We want to imbue our beautiful brown skin with a tinge of brown guilt too! So, please, the next time you need to scapegoat some ethnic minority for a social ill that plagues our great nation, why not give us a try? I volunteer us to take one for the team.

Black Culture

I QUITE LIKE BLACK culture. I just think African Americans have more fun. They're less stuck up than the rest of us. They smile more, laugh harder, place more value in friendship. They have more interesting life stories. We should all strive to appropriate some of that.

Civil Rights

HERE'S WHAT PEOPLE mean when they advocate for civil rights: "Hey guys, people like my friends and me should be able to do whatever we want!!"

Very few people advocate on behalf of a class of people that their friend circle does not contain.

Self-Implicate

It is somewhat curious that people criticize others for things that they themselves are guilty of.

There are various things about which you are supposed to be woke. But ask people who promote these forms of wokeness if they, themselves, follow this wokeness in the confines of their own private thoughts.

Ask a feminist if they harbor any stereotypical views about women. Ask an anti-racist if they harbor any racist reflexes. Ask a vegan if they ever eat butter. Many of us will admit we do.

I say, *that's fine!* Criticize others for that which you are guilty of, too. Frame it as "we should all do better on this, myself very much included."

Racism v. Nationalism

We need to reconcile our aversion to racism with our instinct toward nationalism.

It is considered bad to discriminate against an applicant on skin color, yet it is considered ideal to avoid giving a job to someone overseas. It is considered immoral to let the American poor go sick or hungry, yet no politician vocally supports increases in foreign aid. It's "Buy American!" and not, "Support the global poor!" Explain those dichotomies to me.

Defending Racism

ALL RIGHT—I need to go on a racist rant. Well, not precisely—I would never—but I'd like to do something much worse: defend racism and racists *in general*.

Let's start with this. What specifically is wrong with racism? Generally speaking, racism is a problem because it presupposes that a particular group of people is worth less than another group of people. It is discrimination based on a nebulous notion of ethnicity that has historically been the basis of persecution and subjugation. It's a problem because qualified candidates are declined employment. It's a problem because there is a demonstrable bias toward certain ethnicities in courtrooms. Inasmuch as racism is the most pernicious form of discrimination, then we should call it out as such and condemn it forcefully.

But I'd like to argue that racism is among the *least* pernicious form of discrimination there is.

In practice, it is socially acceptable to value the worth of American lives more than those in other countries, to assume that people living today are worthier of our concern than are people who will live in the future, and to assign a worth of approximately zero to the lives non-human, non-pet animals.

When it comes to caring about these kinds of lives, we aren't particularly moved. And realistically, why should we be? They don't affect anyone like us.

We protest shipping jobs overseas, we ignore global famines, we take vacations by plane, we clear rainforests, and we kill a trillion pounds of meat and fish each year.

I would say that it's normal to casually devalue lives that are far different from ours and to be angered by discrimination directed at those whose lives are similar to our own.

Now, who gets the most worked up about racism? It seems to be people who live in big, racially diverse coastal cities, who went to elite colleges whose student bodies look like the General Assembly of the United Nations, who may be of color themselves—that is, people like me. These people, if I may speak on our behalf, feel that those who reside in homogeneous communities in Middle America don't really care about racial minorities. We feel that these people are *racist*.

And maybe they are; I won't speak on their behalf.

But compare the average 24-year-old white male living in Manhattan to the average 24-year-old black male living in Manhattan. Let's be real—their lives are quite similar. They both take the subway to work. They both have roommates. They both have a nagging feeling that they should pick up the guitar again. They go drinking together. Therefore, when big-city white guy hears about a big-city black guy being singled out by the police, the white guy takes it as a personal affront or at least feels an obligation to express his outrage, lest people think he doesn't care about people like his friends.

Now, think about some town in North Dakota—population 3,840; 3,838 of whom are white and Christian. There are tons of these towns across America. There, the average black guy doesn't exist because none live there. So, when a small-town white guy hears about a black guy being harassed by the NYPD, he isn't particularly moved. And realistically, why should he be? That doesn't affect anyone like him.

In big cities and small towns alike, our friend circles don't contain dirt-poor Somali kids, people living in the year 2422, farm-raised lambs, or nearly extinct Sumatran Rhinoceri.

We can intuit that we are doing them an injustice by carrying on as we are with our institutionalized discrimination toward them. Yet, their lives are so different from ours, so invisible to us, that we give those factions precisely no accord at all. We simply don't care about their supposed plight. We do what the human mind does with criminal ease: dismiss the value of lives that are nothing like our own.

That's why I think it's hypocritical for us big-city liberals to get so worked up about racism. Because buried in our condemnation of racism is the supposition that we, ourselves, recoil in disgust at any hint of bias against those who differ from ourselves. And that just isn't true. That is not what can be deduced from our actions, from our political stances, from our freely stated personal beliefs. We do treat other beings as fundamentally inferior to us so long as they are sufficiently different or distant from us in time, space, or appearance.

When we liberals say that we shouldn't ship jobs overseas, we acknowledge that we value the Vietnamese worker's life less than that of the American worker's. When we permit factory farms to flourish, we acknowledge that raising animals to be tortured and slaughtered is justified by our taste for meat. When we don't prioritize climate change and environmental preservation, we say plainly that the avoidable dramatic mass extinction we are causing isn't worth inconveniencing ourselves to try to avert.

What was so bad about racism? Oh yeah, someone called your friend Sneha a "damn Hindu" and your black buddy Brian got stopped and frisked by the police on his way out of Whole Foods. Am I that coldhearted to say, *who cares?* You *are* Hindu, Sneha! And Brian, you just bought a three-pack of salmon steak; those fish would have loved to have been caught and released.

Here is the real problem and why I'm picking on anti-racism in the first place: my theory is that people can only advocate for two social issues tops. You simply can't be an activist for everything—and, I claim, not realistically for more than two causes.

Maybe racism is indeed the issue most worthy of our outrage. I'll leave that for you to analyze yourself. But, to the extent that you care about activism, to the extent that you believe there's injustice in the world, what I suggest is that you take time to think for yourself about what warrants your attention most. Give special and undue consideration to forms of discrimination that are perpetrated by our silence, that naturally exist in our sympathetic blind spot.

I'll take it further. I say, *let racist attitudes proliferate*. Go ahead: adopt some racist tendencies yourself! But *only if*, whenever someone criticizes you for being racist, you ask your critic why they are so callously discriminatory in their inaction toward third-world poverty, in their ignorance of ethnic persecution, in their snub of future humans who won't have a habitable planet to live on, in their glee when the waiter brings them their medium-rare steak? Why are they so violently hateful toward these groups of intelligent, emotional beings? Why do they treat the individuals in these groups with such blithe disregard? *Isn't it hypocritical to criticize racism if you have much more sinister discriminatory demons in your closet?* If you say all that with utmost sincerity when called out for being racist, I, for one, offer you indefinite immunity from reproach.

To the extent this radical, regressive shift makes activists look inward and direct their outrage toward more objectively devastating forms of discrimination, I have to say, I think that's a win.

carbon-based resentment of humanity

ENVIRONMISANTHROPY

Faith in Humanity

People love anything that absolves them of guilt.

I was watching a video of a manatee stranded on a beach being rescued by a surfer dude who dragged it back to the sea, where it gleefully swam away. How nice, right? "Faith in humanity restored!" people commented on the video robotically. *Finally, something that suggests to us that mankind isn't really a selfish, reckless scourge!*

Really? You're going to base your faith in humanity on a probably staged YouTube clip and ignore the one trillion-odd fish we kill for food every year? You're going to give humanity a pass on the billion odd pounds of plastic we dump in the ocean every year for fish to choke on? Do you realize that of the mammals we have left on this planet, 96% are either human or are currently being raised for human consumption in factory farms? We have eradicated wildlife.

If anything, my faith in humanity goes *down* when I see kind-to-animal human gestures going viral because I can feel the hundred million odd video viewers telling themselves: *You know what? We aren't so bad, us humans. We drag manatees back to sea. We pull straws out of turtles' faces. We clean ducks' feathers after an oil spill. If anything, humans are animals' best friends!*

News flash, humans—you're the scum of the Earth. Your faith in humanity is, at best, misplaced.

Oil

HEY. Have you heard of oil? Like, do you actually know what the fuck oil is?

It was embarrassingly recently that I learned that oil that comes from the ground is decomposed organic material—a.k.a. dead bacteria, plants, and animals whose corpses happened to have never been eaten. It's definitely *not* some naturally occurring chemical that happens to be stuck in the ground as I had once assumed.

Every time you get in a car or fly in a plane, what is it you're burning? The cadavers of canaries, the bark of Birches, among other formerly frolicking, one-time sunbathing beings. It's a wonder we vegans agree to use air travel and plastic at all.

So, given that oil is made up of dead plants and animals [edit: okay, I'm being informed it's almost all dead bacteria {edit: but I'm also being told that bacteria are people, too}], I wondered how much fuel would, say, an uneaten goat produce a million years hence? I looked it up, did the rough math, and was pretty shocked to discover that a 70-pound goat would produce only a half-teaspoon of gasoline! It's just because living things have been dying for so very long that we have so many of their ~~bodies to burn~~ liquefied corpses to incinerate.

In a fuel-efficient car that gets you 30 miles to the gallon, the gas from a goat drives you only 30 yards. That's the length of a tennis court! All the fauna and flora in the San Diego Zoo distill to around a quarter tank of gas! That's so fucked up, if I may say so myself.

A more honest *mpg*, in my view, would be "meters per goat," with the conversion conveniently being that twenty-five miles per gallon equals twenty-five meters per goat.

> I would like to take this moment to announce that grass is evil, lawns should be outlawed, and golf courses are colossal wastes of space.

Infrastructure

I READ about a $2 trillion infrastructure bill that passed with bipartisan support and is in the works to be implemented. But infrastructure is an awfully euphemistic term for theft of property from other species' natural habitats.

Infrastructure means building dams, roads, power lines, and energy plants. A $2 trillion infrastructure package is like building a billion Great Walls and a million Suez Canals smack in the middle of trillions of animals' homes.

Infrastructure gets us places faster, it keeps our air conditioning on; it keeps our water clean; it makes the Internet accessible in remote places. It also wreaks havoc on all else.

> Ugh, anti-straw activists and the free pass they give to plastic cups.

Revolt

IF ANIMALS GOT the news that we were the ones melting their ice caps, chopping down their trees, pumping carbon and pollutants into their oceans, causing the mass extinction of their own and fellow species...they would experience pure, unadulterated rage. They would revolt against the inequity. They would incite an insurrection. They'd peck at our eyeballs; they'd trample our corporate and government offices; they'd go for our literal and figurative jugulars.

It's lucky for us they haven't put the pieces together.

Precious

IT is said that human life is precious. Here's a question: is it?

Here's a life that many seem to live: Be born, go to school, get a job, get a spouse, watch TV in the evenings, give birth, go on bi-annual family vacations, retire, get severely ill, die.

Is that really worth making 50,000 species per year go extinct over?

> I don't trust people who seem fundamentally happy. Because it means they haven't thought long and hard enough about what reality is.

Ecocide

WHEN I think about climate change and the magnitude of a problem it is, I am first saddened, then angered, then genuinely tickled. I can't help but laugh.

And I resent myself for that.

When a problem is so large as to boggle the mind, I find it hard to be anything but amused. Like...

HAHA! I'm an accomplice to stupefying loss of life, calamitous extinction, and figurative bioterrorism! HEHE! I live in literal sin by being a member of the first world! I am the problem! I should be self-hating! I am guilty as charged! But, LOL, I'm self-loving and have no remorse!

Voluntary Human Extinction

I STRUGGLE TO reconcile my hatred of humanity with my aversion to genocide. Damn, I love that opening line.

Anyway, after spending some time Googling this, shall we say, *problem*, I came across an organization whose solution is so ingenious that I'm a little annoyed I didn't think of it first. The organization is The Voluntary Human Extinction Movement ("VHEMT")

The drastic measure VHEMT proposes is the following directive: stop having kids. Just stop. No more babies. *No mas bebés.* 没有孩子了! कोई और बच्चे नहीं!! 素晴らしい. այլեւս երեխաներ չկան!! !!!! لا مزيد من الأطفال

Voluntary extinction will be far more pleasant than the involuntary alternative. Their website, vhemt.org, is straight out of 1993, but their FAQ section is a delight. It politely responds to your pointed objections. I encourage you to read it.

I myself, am less able to be polite on this matter, and I would love to go on a biting rant about how immoral it is to bear children. But I would lose my child-being and child-having audience, so I will refrain* from insulting your mother.

Anyway, again, stop having kids. If you must raise a kid, get one at the human shelter whose entire family died in a house fire or some shit like that.

---

* Okay, okay! I won't refrain! I will oblige! The people have spoken. Here's the anti-child rant you ordered.

<personalrant>Humans are objectively evil and unsustainably numerous, so to create more of them is to commit a crime against humanity and its fellow species. We should shame people who do have kids. We should judge childbirth far more harshly than we treat getting a dog from a pet store. Really, dawg, you got your kid from a baby mill, a.k.a. your or your co-parent's womb? Don't you know there are rescue babies available by the millions from Syria and China, not to mention America and every other corner of the world? Just like getting a dog from a pet store instead of the SPCA effectively gives the death sentence to a dog at the pound, so too does having a baby effectively kill a baby, or at least condemns them to misery. It's like the Toms model got drunk: for every baby you have, we'll let one perish! But it's actually much worse. Given that humans are also carbon-producing factories in regards to their unyielding consumption of carbon&methane-producing goods and services, each kid is probably also sealing the fate of dozens of future kids' premature death due to the contribution they'll make to global warming. According to VHEMT, each child avoided is 37 times better for the planet than going vegan. It is by a very, very wide margin, the best personal change you can make to fight climate change. If you do *nothing* personally for environmental reasons and you blame climate change on governments and corporations, then, actually, good for you! You're logically consistent; please enjoy your guilt-free parenthood—they're so adorable! How old is she? Sixteen months? Awww, so cute! But if you do *anything personally* for the planet—say, recycle, fly less, eat less meat, bring reusable bags to the grocery store, turn off the goddamn lights—and you *still* choose to have children, why call yourself an environmentalist at all? Your selfishness is noted and you admit your activism is purely performative, not at all focused on results.</personalrant>

> If you must have a kid, at least be destitute. The poorer the kid, the less harm they will inflict on the world.

accurate assessment of politics

POLITICUE

> Personal beliefs seem closer to being determined entirely through social influence rather than through entirely personal introspection, which, if true, is ironic.

> I'm a conspiracy theorist conspiracy theorist. My conspiracy theory is that all conspiracy theories are false.

Touchy Subjects

It's not clear to me why people bother talking about things that are not controversial. If everyone agrees with an idea, then why are we talking about it? If everyone rejects an idea, then why are we talking about it? What needs to be worked through is the stuff in the middle.

Poster Boy

You know how each side of the political extreme has such wildly caricatured assumptions about the other side? Conservatives are xenophobic, climate-denying, corporate-brainwashed racists! Liberals are pretentious soy boy beta male cucks who think that gender is a construct, that Christmas is offensive, and that the world is going to end!

But it is actually kind of hard to find those cartoon characters among the general voting population. Everyone is more or less a kind, rational, family-loving person, not remotely resembling the extremists that their political opponents envision.

Everyone, that is, except for me. I think I am the caricature incarnate of the liberal left and I, therefore, apply to be its poster boy.

I *am* a soy boy: I'm vegan and I fucking love tofu and soy milk. Literally, half my meals are Soylent.

I am the assistant vice captain of team beta male! I'm never aggressive, I hate selling, and I readily defer to others' preferences in social situations.

I do declare war on Christmas! *Someone* needs to countervail its transparently commercial hijacking.

I do think gender is a construct! Hell, I think existence, consciousness, free will, and physical matter are constructs, too.

I think marriage is a scam propped up by the wedding industry; hence, I haven't had the opportunity to be a literal cuck. But were I the marrying type, *I don't know*, maybe I'd give cuckoldry a try! It sounds just kinky enough for me.

I do think life on Earth is going to end if we don't slam the brakes on our carbon emissions that figuratively went from 0 to 60 in 1.2 galactic seconds. I do think that even if our species delays its extinction a-whole-'nother millennium, that will *still* be such a devastating disaster of a scenario given how very long life has thrived in this world.

At the time of this book's writing, I am broke, jobless, working on a "startup." I'm in debt and living at my parents' figurative basement. Yet I *still* identify as a coastal elite!

So, conservative right, cast me as your villain! Enlist me as your straw man! Quote this book as evidence of deranged #LiberalLogic. Cite me as evidence that a cuck like me exists.

> We share 99.9% of the same DNA as every other person on the planet. That 0.1%, though, apparently that's irreconcilable.

Come Together

Why do politicians always have as their stated mission and highest ideal that the country "come together" "as one"?

Since when do we as Americans value mass accord and deference to others' points of view? I'm good with division, thank you very much.

With that said, as an aspiring politician myself, I'll fall in line and tell you how *I'll* bring the country together: by pointing out that both sides of the aisle, for all practical purposes, ignore climate change, factory farming, and extreme poverty. And if we're being honest, those interrelated situations are *far* more worth our concern than whatever else we waste our time bickering about.

YOLO

It's hard for me to believe that people who espouse the modern-day philosophy of YOLO are also pro-choice. If you're such a staunch non-believer in reincarnation as your reverence for YOLO would suggest, then what *of* the decision to terminate the one and *only* life a person had to live? If indeed it is true that life is a one-shot deal, a singular opportunity, then surely you must struggle with abortion, philosophically, no? Surely, you must wonder if that opportunity is yours to take away.

I, myself, am pro-choice, very much so. But I, at least, offer the improbability of reincarnation the solemnity it deserves. Which is to say I refrain from invoking *YOLO* to promote reckless behavior.

Pro-Abortion, Not Pro-Choice

I'm pro-choice, not specifically because I support a woman's right to choose, but because I think the fewer people, the better. Is that a deeply fucked-up thing to say? Yes, I do believe it is.

But what I do think is interesting is how vastly different lines of reasoning can conclude the same thing. What do you do when you agree with someone on their conclusion but disagree with how they got there? I think that's an awkward situation in any debate. Because ultimately, you agree, but fundamentally, you seethe.

Diary Entries

5/27/16

OBAMA HUGGED AN OCTOGENARIAN HIROSHIMA SURVIVOR today. I thought it was a nice gesture, but it was a little weird to watch. It would be like if Bin Laden's grandson were to hug a 9/11 survivor in sixty years.

Like, symbolic, I guess, but *yikes*, undeniably weird.

4/18/16

SPACEX LANDED A rocket to be reused for future missions. You should have heard the eruption of cheers from inside the command center at Cape Canaveral. Okay, you know what the cutest thing in the entire world is? It's when extreme nerds get excited about something so objectively important.

It reminded me of the time when the 190 countries finalized an agreement on global climate change legislation, when it was confirmed the Higgs boson particle exists, and when they landed Curiosity on Mars. Those buttoned-up scientists and diplomats were so elated; they displayed the purest, most perfect form of happiness. And the whole world was happy for them.

Excitement around progress around science, technology, and global cooperation is what we should rally around, tailgate on behalf of, have regional identities tied to. To hell with sports and movies.

Veterans' Pay

Dude, what's with the unrestrained adulation heaped upon veterans? They enrolled in a job voluntarily. That job happens to be risky and comes with benefits that must make it worthwhile. End of discussion, right? Wrong; we elevate them to the status of heroes. Why??

———

There is another profession called *saturation diving*. That job involves descending thousands of feet below the surface of the ocean, staying there for weeks in the underwater analogue of a space station, and working on oil rigs or other mega contraptions way down under in treacherous seabed conditions.

The profession involves rigorous training and inflicts high rates of neurological disorders and psychological trauma on its practitioners. Fatal accidents are common; the divorce rate among practitioners is high. Yet, without this profession, we on land wouldn't have many of the luxuries and freedoms we take for granted, namely everything that stems from our use of oil.

There's no national holiday for their fallen; no one thanks them for their service; they're not guests of honor at SOTU addresses. And my guess is that they are perfectly fine with that. Thrilled, even! Why?

Because they make $500,000 per year, and that compensates them for the risks.

———

Here's my theory: The reason we go out of our way to celebrate the military is that we don't want to pay them as much as they deserve for the risk they are taking. If we did pay them market rate for assuming that kind of potential harm, the federal military budget would quickly spiral out of control and we'd go broke as a nation.

So, instead, we say how valiant they are, what gratitude the nation has for their service, what transcendent nobility their profession bestows upon them and their entire families. And we get away with paying them a pittance.

You want to really honor the military? Ditch the Triple-A discounts and lose the medals of honor. Just make their starting salary even a tenth of what saturation divers make.

Couldn't Agree More

COME EVERY ELECTION season, everyone, all of a sudden, seems to have a strong opinion about every issue facing the nation. What I think is actually the case is that no one cares about issues that don't affect them, and to keep discussion about such issues to a minimum, they pick the side of the issue that most people in their community seem to be on. Why? Because that's the viewpoint that will end the conversation fastest.

People around you support gay marriage? *Word, love is love!* People you know think it's an abomination? *Word, thousands of years of tradition has got to be worth something!* Next topic! That's people's true political motivation: to conclude discussions about issues that don't affect them.

Hence, we see an electoral college map that is regionally red and regionally blue, both at a national level and local level. Why? I doubt it's because those regions' genetic pools and economic realities predispose them toward feeling one way or another about issues that only affect others. It might just be that one thing we can all agree on is that the universal strategy to minimize political discussion is to go along with what people around you believe whatever those objectively baseless viewpoints happen to be.

Anyway, let's move on to the next topic, shall we?

Government Overthrow

Did you know that it is a very serious federal criminal offense to "advocate for the overthrow of the US government," punishable by up to 20 years in federal prison per US Penal Code 18 § 2385?

But I object, your honor. Who does the US government think it is telling me what I can and cannot call for? I find this restriction to be a gross limitation of my free speech as an American. It is undue governmental self-preservation, which I would argue is anticompetitive and unconstitutional.

I would like to be the Rosa Parks of my generation. So, I will commit this criminal offense in plain view in an effort to make a change.

I SPECIFICALLY ADVOCATE AND CALL FOR THE OVERTHROW OF THE UNITED STATES' GOVERNMENT. LET US GET THE FEDERAL GOVERNMENT GONE.

Seriously, let's start anew. Maybe we could install a ruling power whose sole mission is to maximize the longevity of intelligent life on Earth. The present system of low gas prices and unending economic growth doesn't work for me. So, I say <u>overthrow the American government!</u> Have I convinced you that this is not some kind of lighthearted joke that my defense lawyer can cast away as patently unserious? That I have called for the overthrow of the American government as loud and clear as I possibly can?

The ball is in your court, *Government*. You know where the fuck I live.

POLITICUE

Entertainer In Chief

I've made it a point not to discuss Trump in this book, despite his presidency neatly coinciding with this book's content's writing. Everyone talks about him all the live-long day and I don't have much to add.

As of January 2020, we're in the middle of the democratic primary. There's a lot of heavy Trump-bashing during these debates; that I can report to you from the past. The bashing is warranted on the guy's policies alone. Climate change denial, not to sound like a broken record, is truly unforgivable.

But I think everyone on those primary debate stages should be required to answer this question: "What about America have you learned from the rise of Donald Trump?" If you can't answer that without using a synonym of "deplorable," then what business do you have bashing him? Clearly, a huge number of Americans really love the guy.

I'll tell you what I learned from him or at least what suspicion I had about the electorate that was confirmed: all else equal, people want the occupant of the Oval Office to be an entertainer.

The POTUS, whoever they are, is constantly in the news. There is always some publicized drama surrounding the commander in chief.

As someone who has forsworn TV, movies, sports, and fiction, I can speak for myself in saying that political drama fills a large portion of my own need for entertainment. *So-and-so said this! So-and-so vetoed that! So-and-so's reaction to this and that was... such and such!* I can't look away.

Fine. It is what it is. But if I'm going to let politics serve as entertainment, then at least a small part of my motivation in picking a president is picking a good entertainer. That is why I think people love Donald Trump. The man is indubitably entertaining.

From a purely entertainment-focused perspective, who would you rather have cast in a feature film that you're forced to watch for four to eight years? Barack or Mitt? Bush or Gore? DJT or HRC? Reagan or whoever the other guy was? Come on, the formers, any day!

Obama: how witty and cerebral! Bush: how downright affable! Clinton: what a fucking G! Trump: dude's an actual stand-up comedian! And in all cases, their political opponents were polished stiffs. People overcomplicate elections. In practice, the more naturally funny candidate wins.

Don't get me wrong. Policy *should* be what you decide on. If Gore had been elected, maybe life on Earth would have had a chance at long-term survival. Had Hill-hill won, surely many, many fewer people would have perished from COVID-19. But at the voting booth, policy, I suspect, is not paramount on swing voters' minds. They're just playing casting director for the country's lead actor.

Nikhil 4 Prezident

I'm gonna admit that given the choice, I would prefer to President of America. Mainly to slap some sense into the masses, among which is you. Here are some things I would smack you around about.

I would legalize animal abuse just to get people talking about animal rights; in particular, to shed light on the atrocities being committed in factory farms. It's shocking to me that people can lament a puppy being kicked when both they and their pup had veal for lunch.

I wouldn't shed crocodile tears whenever there's a minor national tragedy like a mass shooting. Consoler in Chief, my ass. Let's be real. This so-called tragedy resulted in the deaths of seven people. Seven. If we reduced the rate of death from heart disease by one one-tenth of one percent, we would save *600* people a year. The fact that we're not talking about that is the real national tragedy. Oh, you say we can't compare lives like that? Get the fuck out of here with "we can't compare lives like that." My entire political platform rides on the argument that we can.

I would discourage pregnancy. Miracle of life, my ass. More like *couldn't keep your dick in your pants or resist the evolutionary brainwashing that is the maternal urge, could you?* Each kid is a carbon-producing factory that will indisputably contribute to killing scores of future people and will result in tens of thousands of animals being raised and killed for the satiation their cooked muscles provide.

"Fuck bringing people, *especially Americans*, into this world," I'd tell America without a hint of irony. Child tax credit? Try child tax *debit*. My position on gay marriage? No marriage. All marital unions declared null and void. Be free, people!

I would remove the tax-deductibility of domestic charitable giving. Charity starts abroad if I have any say. America's poor are the global upper-middle. I would quintuple the spending on foreign aid. What we contribute is pathetic to the point of comedy, and it's shocking to me that no candidate, even the most left-leaning, puts this argument forth.

I'd go nuts with cutting carbon emissions. Planes grounded. Cars abolished. Beef criminalized. Medals of freedom only given to those whose contributions to science maximally reduce the parts per million of carbon in the air.

I'd encourage shipping jobs overseas because foreign people's lives are not worth *that much* less than Americans'.

This book would, against all of my advisors' advice, serve as my political platform.

At the very least, I would stand out as a candidate among a sea of thumb-pointing parrots.

justifying hate & atrocity for the greater good

UTILITARIOFASCISM

Likeness Monster

The more similar you are to me, the more I value your life.

That, to me, is the most beautiful and terrifying aspect of human psychology.

Justice for Some

HEY. Do you believe in equality? Do you *really, truly* believe in equality? If not, please skip to the last paragraph.

But if so, then please define equality. Equality among whom?

Does that definition include a child sex slave in India? If not, please skip to the last paragraph.

But if so, then why don't I hear her story in the conversation about #MeToo?

⇨ You're a bigot.

Deep Breadth

THE BROADER YOUR prejudice, the more socially acceptable it is. I can hate humans in general but not Mongols in particular; dogs in general but not Poodles in particular; meat in general but not bacon in particular. It's as if what we're offended by is not hatred per se, but rather the singling out of a specific thing to hate.

Diffuse Responsibility

Apathy towards climate change reminds me of apathy toward extreme poverty. It goes something like this:

It's not my fault, it's unlikely to affect me, and anything I do personally won't make a difference in the scheme of things. Insofar as I should bear some responsibility, so should everyone else. I don't see them doing anything, so I won't either.

That makes me sad, even more so when I catch myself employing that same line of reasoning to excuse my own lack of contributions to the causes.

How I Can Be So Heartless

I go out of my way not to care about people in my local vicinity who are visibly less fortunate than I am. Because I know I live in one of the richest square miles in the world. So, my local plight couldn't possibly matter.

Holocaust Believer

SLAVERY AND THE Holocaust are entirely unsurprising when we consider that you and I currently ignore widespread malnutrition, child prostitution, the climate crisis, ethnic cleansing, labor camps, commercial deforestation, industrial factory farming among many other sickening atrocities currently being committed by our fellow humans on a dizzying scale.

We bury our heads, claiming it isn't specifically our fault, that this is just how an imperfect world operates. We turn the same blind eye that the most culpable bystanders in all of human history have turned as well.

> Here's a depressing belief I admit to thinking has potential legitimacy: while there exists extreme suffering in the world and the prospect of much more in the future, the pursuit of happiness is immoral.

Effective Altruism

I must admit that I'm part of a cult, and I would be remiss not to give it a plug as being that which you, too, should accept as your Lord & Savior. The organization is the Effective Altruism (EA) movement, and our disciple is Peter Singer. But brace yourself because EA's tenets are a little radical.

EA says we should use numbers and logic, not emotion and compassion, to determine who and what is worthy of our concern and how is best to help.

Let's say your concern is the issue of hunger. You can buy some groceries from Safeway and give them to the homeless person you walk past on your way to work and have your heart filled with the gratitude on his face. Or you can take the cash from your would-be grocery bill, and send it to UNICEF, or another GiveWell-approved charity with the belief that the organization you pick will put the money to better use in some far-flung country you'd never consider visiting. The EA cult member would do some back-of-the-envelope calculations, and if she concluded that the latter were more effective, she'd put her heartstrings aside and do the fucking latter.

Untitled

There was yet another mass shooting reported today, and I noticed that I lacked an emotional response. There are so many of them these days that I've become desensitized. Which is embarrassing to admit, even to myself. Which made me wonder if I should make myself care about mass shootings or if I should live my life not being affected by reports of them. Which made me realize that we should wonder that about any world problem we have or lack a visceral reaction to.

It is said that there is a war on Christmas. Do I care? No. Should I care? No. Animals in factory farms are killed very young. Do I care? Yes, that's so sad. Should I care? Not specifically about their age because in practice, letting them live longer is even worse for the environment. Word has it global warming is a problem. Do I expect that problem to affect me, personally? Not really; I have plenty of privilege to keep me safe. Should I care about the issue? Yes, obviously, I should care about nothing more.

We should make explicit the consideration of what is and is not worthy of our outrage. Our gut is notoriously unreliable as an analysis machine.

On Being Nice

I'M A DICK, and that allows me to be a good person. That is the subject of today's lecture.

Let's say we like ladybugs, and you must choose between killing one ladybug and two ladybugs, and you choose to kill two. Are you a bad person? Yes. Given the choice, you should have killed one; you should have chosen the action that caused the least harm, prevented the most harm. Let's say you can feed one hungry person or ten hungry people for the same cost and you choose to feed only one. Are you a bad person? Yes. You should have fed ten, you definitionally bad person!

Okay, now let's say you can cure 10 poor Africans' diseases or you can cure one American's disease and you choose the one American. Are you a bad person? "Well, now, hold on," you might say. "I guess that depends on how you compare the worth of Africans' lives to the worth of Americans' lives."

Am I somewhat partial to my fellow Americans? Sure. If pressed, I might even value an American 2:1 compared to a Somali's life. But I don't value American's lives 10:1, 100:1, let alone 1000:1. Yet, 1000 to 1 is basically how I see "nice people" making decisions when it relates to people into whose fellow-American eyes they can look versus impoverished people on the other side of the world they will, under no circumstance, ever encounter.

If you, a well-meaning philanthropist, put $10,000 toward a scholarship for an underprivileged American when you could have given that same 10 Gs to

UTILITARIOFASCISM

Malaria prevention efforts that would have *prevented the death of many young children*, are you a good person? I must say *au contraire*, you bad, *bad* guy.

The problem is that the conventional method of assessing how nice someone is, how little of a dick they are, is observing how they treat the people around them. Are they polite to the waiter? Kind to their parents? Giving in their communities? Supportive of the arts? Doing those things is what makes people conventionally nice and not at all a dick.

But when you choose to do something nice at the expense of something far nicer, you are, by the definition you and I already negotiated, a quintessential bad person, dare I say an evil, depraved sociopath.

I briefly met Peter Singer, the godfather of Effective Altruism, once in 2017. My one question was if he thought an effective altruist could ever be the president of America. He laughed *at* me, and said, "No way. Look at who we have in office now." But I'm still not so sure. I think that the liberal analogue of Trump looks a lot like an EA and has a similar shot at breaking through the noise. And I know just the candidate to fill that role: me.

Kid in a Cage

AN IDEA I had in college was to commit many first-degree felonies in order to prove a point. It was a thought experiment not an actual plan so please chill out. It was part of an essay that I submitted to a university-wide essay contest and I won $500 for my essay "On Inaction" which you can Google to see where my head was at, at age 19.

At the time, I was very sad about the situation of third-world poverty. Why was seemingly no one up in arms about the preventable deaths happening by the millions in parts of the world whose people don't have access to sufficient food, water, healthcare, women's rights, education, shelter?

Everyone around me seems rich and clearly has the resources to prevent many of those far-away deaths, yet... no one does and no one cares? Why is that so different from murder? Having education about poverty and doing nothing about it feels like the malicious element of premeditation to me.

My assessment was that the reason for the indifference was because the concepts of permission of death and murder are treated as fundamentally distinct in people's minds, a distinction we all take for granted from a very young age. Yet, inaction that fails to prevent death is equivalent to murder in its outcome: someone died who would not have died had your personal decisions been different.

I came up with this thought experiment as a proposed publicity stunt for this maniacal, but important, point of view:

UTILITARIOFASCISM

I would fly to some remote village in some landlocked, geopolitically irrelevant third world country and I would ask to see a child clearly on his last days, you know, dying of malnutrition, malaria, or other classic extreme-poverty-kid cause of death. And when no one was looking, I would abduct the kid.

I'd charter a private jet, bribe the local officials on both ends to look the other way. I would arrive in the Big Apple with the terrified, ailing child.

Back in New York, I would have devised a 5-foot wide cube made of clear, dense, impenetrable glass with a door and an unbreakable lock. I would put the kid in the cage, lock the door, melt the key and haul the box to Washington Square Park, where I'd leave it. I'd go home and turn on the news.

There would be a starving kid in a cage at the center of global wealth.

At first, people would assume this contraption was just some street performance, maybe an escape act of sorts. But then people would see the look of desperation on the kid's face; they would take note of his emaciation. *He can't be so much better of a method actor than me*, the Tisch-student passersby would reason. Once the door proves unopenable, well-meaning millionaires would flood emergency services with *911* calls. Swat teams would clear the area, a tactical team of specialists would be summoned to open the cage. But that polycarbonate cube will not open, just as I had planned. Eventually, the child would perish. Rescue efforts would cease. After all, he was terribly ill, he didn't have access to medicine or clean water and it was scorching hot where he was left to die. It would be headline news for days; NYPD and FBI investigations would commence.

Security footage and eyewitnesses would lead the authorities to my door, guns drawn. I'd surrender. I'd plead innocent and act shocked that I'm being charged at all. I'd offer to represent myself in court. My argument? I didn't kill the kid; I just let him die. Isn't that your argument for the 10 million kids like him who die every year of the same causes of death as a direct result of your explicit choice not to donate or lift a finger in any way? Isn't that the outcome everyone in this courtroom is further guaranteeing for billions more who will be born into a climate-ravaged future that is in no small part of our making?

After a long, internationally publicized trial, I submit my closing arguments to the jury thusly:

Had I left the kid where he was, he would have suffered the same fate. Any one of you could have wired him fifty bucks to get him some proper nutrition and nurse him back to health. Explain to me what makes me more complicit than you. Is it that I changed his latitude and longitude to a local coordinate, and that makes his life feel more real to you? Is it that I failed to be the Good Global Samaritan that you also failed to be?

Members of the jury, through this stunt, I have successfully conflated in much of the public's minds the traditionally polar concepts of murder and permission of death. And maybe that, I would conclude, *will save more lives than the one I took.*

final meta meta meta meta meta arguments

EPILOGIC

Dark Thoughts

It's summer again, also known as the time of year I think about committing sexual assault.

Now, *whoa, hold on, let me explain.*

First of all, I'm a man and don't claim to be free of male shittiness. For example, if I see a woman on the subway platform whose posterior I find endearing, I'll think to myself, *damn girl, I'd like to bite your butt!* I might even imagine myself performing this act. And then I'll think about something else. I will have made certain that no one sees me sneaking the split-second peek.

It is technically true that I would like to bite that butt. But, I obviously would never do such a thing outside the confines of, say, an intimate, consensual buttbiting relationship. It should go without saying I would never remotely consider *doing* such a thing to a stranger on a subway platform. *That's sexual assault.*

But I did have the thought. I had a fleeting contemplation of an act that would legally constitute molestation. Mega yikes. So, that's abhorrent, right?

...Right??

Well, maybe not. In considering my heinous thought, I actually think it might be totally fine. I have even felt comfortable sharing this, not to mention all of my other dark, vile, bigoted private thoughts with you here in this book. Why??

Because, dear reader, I have it on tremendous authority that you, in the onfines of your own mind, have disturbingly dark thoughts, too.

EPILOGUE

> As a bigot, I would like to reclaim the word "bigot." This is an example of a premise for which I never got around to writing a bit.

Correct Me If You're Wrong

I was watching a news clip of a cable news anchor—it was one of those Andersen Cooper, Don Lemon types—interviewing some high-ranking White House official, like National Security Advisor or something. To clarify some point, the reporter began his question with, "Now, correct me if you're wrong, but..."

It was clearly misspoken. He meant to say *if I'm wrong*, but *if you're wrong* came out. The intent was clarification, not repudiation. Neither party noticed the slip-of-tongue, the government official confirmed the clarification, and the interview went on.

But I sat there dumbfounded.

Did he just say what I thought he said? Was that implicit condescension uttered to one of the most powerful people in the world? I rewound the clip a dozen times, and there it was, said clearly, "correct me if you're wrong..."

Wow, I thought. *What a preemptive nuclear strike. What a presumptuous rhetorical shot. What an unequivocal declaration of pure confidence in that which one knows to be controversially true.*

If you don't have any fringe beliefs, you're a blind conformist, which, fine, fair enough. But if you do have some fringe beliefs, then you had better be ready to go to battle on their behalf at a moment's notice. *Here's what I have to say, and I fucking dare you to challenge me on it, you wrongheaded nincompoop!* is the go-to vibe.

I, like most, tend to let others' negative reactions to my beliefs make me believe in them less and stay silent about them. But here, out of nowhere came a declaration, which, if internalized, could serve as a mantra with which I could lead my life: *correct me if you're wrong.*

That, I thought, is *what people need to hear in my voice, see in my eyes, feel in my very presence.*

Shiiiiit, I thought, *that's what I should name my fucking book if I ever write one.*

Index O'Essays

∞≠8   193
10 Commandments 257
Brasierrr..........34
Would You Rather.....35
Retraction.......35
Personals........36
Ex-Girlfriends..36
4.0 Eyes..........222
Always a Probability 161
Analogy..........134
And, Scene......17
Animalien........80
Ascetic............66
Aspiration.......46
Attorney In-Law 92
Bad Words......96
Base 10..........168
Be Confident.130
Beats & Words 88
Belated Introduction..7
Best Friend...Forever?
.................175
Best Life..........49
Billie...............109
Bit of Both.....167
Black Culture.285
Blackout History 196
Blasphemy....255
Bloody Hancock 68
Breakup Advocacy....57
Brown Privilege 284
Browser Clutter 45

But I'm a Creep 18
Can't Stop, Won't Stop
.................135
Childhood, on VHS....55
Chord.............106
Circumlocution 95
Civil Rights.....285
Classified...........6
Cleanliness......26
Coconut..........72
Coffee Shop......2
Cognitive Puppy 223
College Subway Ads 142
Come Together 305
Comfy............128
Co-opted.......140
Correct Me If You're
  Wrong..........333
Coughing Involuntarily
.................210
Couldn't Agree More
.................310
Dance Party of One 102
Dark at Night...37
Dark Thoughts 332
Deadline;.........57
Deadweight Loss 138
Death Row Dignity..268
Deep Breadth 319
Defeating ISIS 255
Defending Racism...287
Diary Entries..307

Diffuse Responsibility
.................320
Distant..........192
Dizzy.............195
DJ Anxiety.....104
Dog Ears........104
Dreams or Lies? 207
Ecocide.........298
Effective Altruism 322
Encouraging Idiocy...56
Entertainer In Chief.312
Entitlement.....62
Etymology.......81
Experiencing Vice 150
Facile.............96
Faith in Humanity 294
Fast Forward...19
Fiction & Addiction..154
Fiery..............195
Fines.............136
First Time's a Charm.88
Forgetting.....219
Forgiving.......234
Genetic Code Transfer
.................198
Good Luck Purge 97
Government Overthrow
.................311
Gravity..........194
Grievance........95
Growin' Up......56
Heat Vents....200

Hipster Honeybees...76
Holocaust Believer..321
Hostage Situation 178
How I Can Be So
  Heartless.....320
Human Resources....28
Hundapacent 160
Identity Assignment 235
If A Tree Falls.232
Imaginary Girlfriend.21
Imprecision...164
In Exponentiation, I
  Trust...........246
Independence 176
Infrastructure 296
Inside Inside Joke 224
Internal Thought Police
.................224
Internet Stalkers 44
Interspecies Equality
.................264
Involuntary....231
Irrefutabable..254
Irrelevant Delta 137
Itemization....134
Justice for Some 319
Juxtapose......266
Kid in a Cage..326
Let Freedom Ring 180
Life and...?.....230
Life in an Evening 58
Likeness Monster 319

LinkedIn Congrats 45	Parallax 199	Self-Medi(c/t)ating . 149	The XX - Intro 105
Listen Carefully 47	Passing Strangers 24	Self-Reflection 77	Time Delta 116
Logical Lulling 206	Peeing Standing Up. 115	Semicolon....... 89	Time Scales... 242
Long-Winded Diss ... 177	Perennial 275	Send It Back.... 28	Time Traveling 244
Loquacious 20	Pet Food....... 270	Sex-Ed 52	Touchy Subjects 303
Marijuana Addict 146	Pick-Up Line.... 19	Shun Contraception 199	Try the Opposite 124
Marriage Dissidence 174	Poetic 90	Side Effects Be Damned 148	Two-Page Memoir .. 185
Mental Connections 223	Positive Negative EV 165		Uber Drivers ... 45
Mental FM.... 101	Poster Boy 303	Sign to Leave 114	Unfortunate . 113
Metasongnition 103	Precious 297	Snitches of the Soul .. 16	Uninformed.. 196
Microkin 197	Preempting Criticism .. 5	So Humbled.... 73	Unsubscribe ... 47
Misdeeds........ 65	Pro-Abortion, Not Pro-Choice 306	Socialism 137	Untitled........ 323
Music These Days 107		Solipsism 231	Veganic Confidence 265
Name That Song 102	Pronoun Preference.. 94	Spin 101	Veterans Day 308
Naming Conventions. 91	Psychology Theory of Everything.. 217	Spoiler.......... 201	Virtual Reality 234
Nausea 147		Squeaker the Squatter 76	Virtuosic Typing 53
News Addiction 275	Quick Plug: UrRong.com 11		Voluntary Human Extinction... 298
News Reporters 274		Star 67	
Nikeel 92	Racism v. Nationalism 286	Star-Struck.... 192	War on Christianity. 256
Nikhil 4 Prezident 314		State Your Claim 141	Wedding Vows 176
None Taken .. 125	Realization.... 271	Stereotype A... 30	Welcoming ... 283
Nontruth 129	Recapitulating Prev. Essay 243	Stoic 127	What Is? 201
Notoriety........ 65		Story Junkie 9	What the News Is 276
Objectifying Women 118	Retraction 25	Street Smart . 162	When 2 > 3 91
	Revolt........... 297	Sum Ting Wong 66	Where Is You? 225
Oil 295	Rich Dad, Present Dad 55	Sunk Cost 204	Word from Your Host 184
Old Age Meat 267		Swings.......... 124	
On Being Nice 324	Risk, Reworded 134	T's Gone Cold . 70	XY Emotion... 115
One-Sided....... 27	RUOK?.......... 166	Talk Faster...... 29	Y Combinator 135
Only Child 52	Sales Projections 8	Telekinesis.... 221	YOLO 306
Opinion Irrelevance .. 29	Sample Bias 64	Test the Limits 112	Z-Axis 79
Oppojeet 93	Second-Hand Accent. 53	Texting 44	
Oscar-Worthy 205	Secular OMG 254	Than Previously Thought...... 197	
Overpriced.... 139	Self-Implicate 286		

Made in United States
North Haven, CT
26 July 2023